# Business Process Management of Japanese and Korean Companies

**Monden Institute of Management: Japanese Management and International Studies**     (ISSN: 1793-2874)

**Editor-in-Chief:** Yasuhiro Monden *(Mejiro University, Japan)*

Published

Monden Institute of Management
Japanese Management and International Studies – Vol. 5

# Business Process Management of Japanese and Korean Companies

*editors*

**Gunyung Lee**
*Niigata University, Japan*

**Masanobu Kosuga**
*Kwansei Gakuin University, Japan*

**Yoshiyuki Nagasaka**
*Konan University, Japan*

**Byungkyu Sohn**
*Sookmyung Women's University, Korea*

 **World Scientific**

NEW JERSEY · LONDON · SINGAPORE · BEIJING · SHANGHAI · HONG KONG · TAIPEI · CHENNAI

*Published by*

World Scientific Publishing Co. Pte. Ltd.

5 Toh Tuck Link, Singapore 596224

*USA office:* 27 Warren Street, Suite 401-402, Hackensack, NJ 07601

*UK office:* 57 Shelton Street, Covent Garden, London WC2H 9HE

**British Library Cataloguing-in-Publication Data**
A catalogue record for this book is available from the British Library.

ISBN-13 978-981-283-860-5
ISBN-10 981-283-860-0

Typeset by Stallion Press
Email: enquiries@stallionpress.com

Printed in Singapore.

# Japan Society of Organization and Accounting

## Mission of JSOA and Editorial Information

For the purpose of making a contribution to the business and academic communities, the Japan Society of Organization and Accounting (JSOA), a reformed and expanded organization from the Monden Institute of Management, is committed to publishing the book series, entitled *Japanese Management and International Studies*, with a refereed system.

Focusing on Japan and Japan-related issues, the series is designed to inform the world about research outcomes of the new "Japanese style management system" developed in Japan. It includes the Japanese version of management systems developed abroad. In addition, it publishes research by foreign scholars and concerning foreign systems that constitute significant points of comparison with the Japanese system.

Research topics included in this series are management of organizations in a broad sense (including the business group) and the accounting that supports the organization. More specifically, topics include business strategy, organizational restructuring, corporate finance, M&A, environmental management, business models, operations management, managerial accounting, financial accounting for organizational restructuring, manager performance evaluation, remuneration systems, and management of revenues and costs. The research approach is interdisciplinary, which includes case studies, theoretical studies, normative studies and empirical studies, but emphasizes real world business.

Each volume contains the series title and a book title which reflects the volume's special theme.

Our JSOA's board of directors has established an editorial board of international standing, which is served by the Monden Institute of Management. In each volume, guest editors who are experts on the volume's special theme serve as the volume editors.

# Editorial Board

# Contents

# Preface

Business Process Management (BPM) refers to "the control and management of transactions between organizations both within and outside corporations by viewing the transaction flows as processes, which is enabled by breaking up the traditional walls between organizations, sharing information and resources among them, and combining and connecting their transactions".

Today we are experiencing major environmental changes which are characterized by the development of internet and the cut-throat competition between firms. The availability of abundant information and fierce competition among suppliers have made the bargaining power shift from suppliers to buyers and consumers. Consequently, firms began to feel the need to evaluate their performance from the view point of customers, and BPM was considered to be a right answer to these needs. The concern for BPM has increased due to the IT innovation where the has visualization of business processes and the sharing of information become possible. However, recent research on BPM has put too much focus on the visualization of business process by using IT. We believe that the research on BPM must be linked with the existent management tools.

This book focuses on how to build BPM as a management model, addressing the importance of BPM views, the effectiveness of its approach, and the research trend of BPM. This book also includes the survey results of Japanese and Korean companies' BPM practices and case studies of Japanese and Korean companies. In summary, the purpose of this book is to construct and discuss a BPM model based on oriental views.

Let us now briefly consider how such intentions are specifically presented in each part of this volume.

## Part 1. Theory and Framework of BPM

In Part 1, a priority is given to clarify the theoretical aspects of the basic BPM structure. This part begins with the framework of BPM model, followed by various theoretical aspects of BPM including business process innovation under varying conditions, the management information used in BPM, and the influence of global environments.

The first paper in Part 1 starts the discussion by dividing BPM into two fragments — a *process management* and a *process strategy*. This paper provides the framework about how to understand, construct, manage and evaluate business processes both inside and outside corporations so that the customers are satisfied.

The second paper aims at accomplishing following ideas in practical business: by linking BPM and actual cost accounting based on ABC with latest information technology, timely controlling the operation of the field and cost-accounting for financial accounting; and at the same time, verifying cost related to management indicators in order to ensure profitable products.

The third paper overviews the current situation and challenges captured in Small and Medium-Sized Enterprises (SMEs) network, looking at the network as a business process, and exploring the significance of managing the SMEs' business processes within such a network.

The fourth paper discusses how global process management in the enterprises is executed and what issues must be considered. Moreover, it examines the methods for managing global processes across corporations.

## Part 2. Case Studies on BPM in Japanese and Korean Companies

Part 2 consists of four papers on BPM practices in Japanese and Korean companies — *Panasonic Corporation, Nagahama Canon* (a subsidiary of Canon Inc), *LG Electronics,* and *Korea Telecommunication.* Based on the BPM model, each paper reports the results from the case studies carried out during 2003–2008. They attempt to reveal the present state of BPM practices in Japan and Korea.

The first paper in Part 2 summarizes the main points of the research results from the case study on the BPM practices in *Panasonic Corporation* of Japan and explores how and why Panasonic Corporation has been pursuing *Business Process Innovations* so actively.

The second paper explores the factors enabling *Nagahama Canon management* to gain the understanding and cooperation of the workers and successfully implement a new BPM system in the company.

The third paper presents a case study concerning the management system and BPM introduction process of *LG Electronics* of Korea, which was performed during the site visit in 2006. In this paper, the BPM system of this company is discussed, and the structure of its process management is examined.

The fourth paper highlights the application of BPM in service business by studying *Korea Telecommunication* (KT). It shows how BPM supports the corporate vision and strategy. The paper begins by reviewing the background and the phases of introducing BPM in the company. Then, it presents the overall system of KT's BPM and how two illustrative processes selected among many are implemented.

## Part 3. Empirical Study of BPM in Japanese and Korean Companies

In this part, the results from surveying companies in Japan and Korea about BPM practices are analyzed and the characteristics as well as their differences in BPM practices are discussed. Furthermore, based on the survey, it attempts to provide insights on how the degree of process reform influences enterprise value in Japanese and Korean companies.

The first paper in Part 3 presents the current status of process management in both countries as in 2004, which focused particulary on the relationships between process innovation and those factors such as customer participation and competitive factor in Japanese and Korean companies.

The second paper discusses the relationship between the degree of process reform and its outcomes based on the survey results of Japanese and Korean companies regarding BPM. Particularly, the categorical regression analysis with the framework of Balanced Scorecard (BSC) has been performed and the causal relationship between the degree of process reform and its effects is verified.

The editors are very grateful to Ms. Yvonne Tan, the commissioning editor of World Scientific Publishing Company for her various invaluable efforts to make this volume a reality. Ms. Bhupathiraju Shalini Raju, the production editor, is also much appreciated for handling our manuscript. Furthermore, I would like to express special thanks to

Prof. Yasuhiro Monden, the founder of Monden Institute of Management, who made it possible for us to publish this book as book series Vol. 5 of the institute.

Finally, the authors who worked for this volume will be amply rewarded if it contributes new ideas or knowledge to the literature on business management, information management, and Asian management, thereby being of some use to people around the world.

Gunyung Lee
*Editor-in-Chief*
*October 2009*

# List of Contributors

**Satoshi Arimoto**
Associate Professor
Faculty of Economics, Niigata University
8050 Ikarashi 2-no-cho, Niigata City
950-2181 Japan
E-mail: s.arimoto@econ.niigata-u.ac.jp

**Yoko Asakura**
Associate Professor
Department of Economics and Finance
Faculty of Business
Osaka International University
3-50-1 Sugi, Hirakata, Osaka
573-0192 Japan
E-mail: badc9081@mis.oiu.ac.jp

**Asako Kimura**
Associate Professor
Faculty of Business Administration
Kansai University
3-3-35 Yamatecho, Suita City, Osaka
564-8680 Japan
E-mail: asakmr@ipcku.kansai-u.ac.jp

**Masanobu Kosuga**
Professor, School of Business Administration
Kwansei Gakuin University
1-1-155 Uegahara, Nishinomiya, Hyogo
662-8501 Japan
E-mail: masa-kos@kwansei.ac.jp

**Gunyung Lee**
Professor, Faculty of Economics
Niigata University
8050 Ikarashi 2-no-cho, Niigata City
950-2181 Japan
E-mail: lee@econ.niigata-u.ac.jp

**Toshiyuki Nagasaka**
Professor, Faculty of Business Administration
Konan University
8-9-1 Okamoto, Higashinada-ku
Kobeshi, Hyougo, 658-8501 Japan
E-mail: nagasaka@konan-u.ac.jp

**Keisuke Sakate**
Associate Professor
Faculty of Business Administration
Osaka University of Commerce
4-1-10 Mikuriyasakaemachi, Higashiosaka, Osaka
577-8505 Japan
E-mail: sakate@daishodai.ac.jp

**Byungkyu Sohn**
Professor
Department of Management
College of Business Administration
Sookmyung Women's University
Yongsan-gu Chongpadong 2-ga 53-12
Seoul, Korea
E-mail: bksohn@sookmyung.ac.kr

**Ryuta Uematsu**
Representative, Opt. u.
3-5-37 Minamioizumi, Nerima-ku, Tokyo
178-0064 Japan
E-mail: ryuta-uematsu@spn1.speednet.ne.jp

**Naoya Yamaguchi**
Associate Professor, Faculty of Economics
Niigata University
8050 Ikarashi 2-no-cho, Niigata City
950-2181 Japan
E-mail: naoya@econ.niigata-u.ac.jp

# PART 1

# THEORY AND FRAMEWORK OF BPM

# 1

# The Conceptual Framework of Business Process Management

Gunyung Lee

*Niigata University, Japan*

## 1  Introduction

It is generally known that today's era — the IT era — is characterized by the global spread of information networks using Information Technology and the Internet. In the IT era, corporate activities both inside and outside the corporation, are conducted in multiple areas simultaneously and surpass the hitherto existing limits of time and space. Because of this historical background and the complete environmental change to cut-throat competition, the leadership in commercial deals has shifted from suppliers to buyers. Consequently, the suppliers' appropriate response to buyers' and customers' demands becomes one of the primary means to achieve a competitive advantage. Hence, in order to respond to the power wielded by customers (buyers and end-users), the suppliers need to customize their products and services according to the customers' tastes and desires to cater to the likes of each customer.

It is necessary to (i) move the managerial point from the conventional vertical communication system usually found in organizations to a horizontal communication system and (ii) establish a Business Process Management (BPM) system that can speedily and flexibly manage its responses to such environmental changes. This paper will discuss a framework that incorporates the understanding, construction, management, and evaluation of the business process, both inside and outside the corporation such that the customers are satisfied in a competitive environment in the IT era.

## 2  Necessity and Possibility of Process Management in the IT Era

We live in a fast-paced world where things are constantly changing; therefore, it is increasingly difficult to predict what will happen in the near future. Moreover, the development of information that allows one to circumnavigate the limits of time and space on global business transactions has been altering the corporate environment in various ways. This environmental change necessitates that companies swiftly match the input of environmental changes with corporate output. In particular, because of the traditional response which focuses on functions often results in an accumulation of information and materials due to the imbalance among functions and the barriers among the many functions, there is a need for a swift response to the environmental changes from the process management perspective. In the IT era, the necessity of and possibilities for process management are being propounded simultaneously by the following two demands (Monden *et al.*, 2007, pp. 235–248).

## 2.1 *Demand from the management side*

The leadership in commercial deals has shifted from vendors to customers due to the easy access to the Internet and cut-throat competition, and hence, a company needs to plan and offer its products or services in line with the customers' views. In other words, there is a need for horizontal organization management that considers the customer as the starting point. In addition, in Japan, the "Internal Control System (J-SOX Law)" enforced in April 2008 laid down several stipulations regarding operation flow which have to be met. These demands from the management side can be attained by a system that integrates material flow and information flow. Therefore, the construction of a BPM system that can manage the performance of the business process when the customer's view is deemed most valuable as an important means to cater to the demands from the management side.

## 2.2 *Support from innovation in IT*

In the 1990s, Business Process Reengineering (BPR) approaches that tried to achieve a drastic restructuring of the business process using IT, failed because they were unable to obtain the expected support from IT. In the later half of the 1990s, information management using Enterprise Resource Planning (ERP) originated as a result of the failure of these BPR approaches. However, ERP confined the operations into a concrete box, which was unable to support the changing operation flow. Hence, in the 2000s, (i) Service Oriented Architecture (SOA) technology that has enabled the restructuring of the IT environment to allow it to respond more flexibly to the environmental changes and (ii) software (e.g., Savvion, ARIS, and VISIO) that has enabled to support the changing operation flow flexibly have been developed. These are effective tools for the construction of BPM system because these new abilities can be exercised to create the business process and assess real-time performance management virtually.

## 3   History of Business Process Management

As long as the term BPM refers to the management of the business process of horizontal organization, we can say that the origin of process management dates back to the Tailorist approaches. On the other hand, it is said that the trigger that led to the recognition of BPM in Europe and the US was the Total Quality Management (TQM) approach adopted in the 1980s (Jeston and Nelis, 2006, pp. xii–xvi). In the 1990s, European and American companies faced a stagnant market and cut-throat competition across the globe. This led to further development of the ideas of traditional process management, and new methods such as BPR and Six Sigma emerged. BPR was suggested by Hammar in 1990. His article "Don't automate, obliterate" in the Harvard Business Review (July–August 1990) was the starting point from which BPR disseminated quickly. Although BPR aimed to drastically restructure the business process using IT, IT was unable to describe and support the complicated processes (Jeston and Nelis, 2006, pp. xii–xvi).

Drawing upon the lessons learned from the failure of BPR, ERP was introduced in the later half of the 1990s. It appeared as though ERP had already solved the process management problem related to IT; however, ERP was unable to support process improvement because it suffered from many shortcomings including non-flexibility, despite of the fact that it was sold with the catchphrase "best practice". In other words, after ERP was set up, the flexibility of the process was lost and could be likened to dry concrete, even though initially (before installation), ERP was as flexible as wet cement (Smith and Fingar, 2007, p. 73).

There are two opinions regarding the origin of BPM. One is that it originated in the 1990s (Jeston and Nelis, 2006, pp. xii–xvi) and the other is that it emerged after the year 2000 (Jeston and Nelis, 2006; Smith and Finger, 2007). However, it seems that the difference between these two opinions arises from (i) the time frame of the emergence of IT that supports process management and (ii) the history of process management. The latter viewpoint emphasizes IT innovation that supplements the lack of flexibility in ERP. This viewpoint treats BPM according to the development of the Business Process Management System (BPMS), i.e., as a total management system of business process that supports a flexible unity between business process and IT. However, a consensus regarding the content of BPM has yet to be reached and BPM has been reduced to a three–letter acronym used to refer to process management. This paper will discuss a new framework of BPM that is based on its historical progress.

## 4 The Concept of Process

A process is a series of interlinked activities that achieve a specific objective (Daly and Freeman, 1997, p. 16). Davenport (1993, p. 5), however, defines the process as follows: "A process is simply a structured, measured set of activities designed to produce a specified output for a particular customer or market". Therefore, we can say that the definition of process differs with each person. This is the reason why each writer defines the process differently, on the basis of the measurement unit, categorization, and extent of the process.

This study regards the process as "a flow composed of various mutually-dependent groups of activities toward the creation of customer value, the input and the output of which are clearly distinguished, and which have a hierarchical structure depending on the levels of the subject matters of management". In addition, it is necessary for the process to satisfy the following three key elements as explained in Statements on Management Accounting (2000, p. 8).

Transformation: By means of one or more changes, it provides output from a group of interrelated work activities that is of greater value than the inputs.

Feedback control: Involves some regulatory means by which the transformation activities are modified or collected to maintain certain attributes of the output.

Repeatability: Implies that a process is executed many times in the same manner.

## 5  Process Classification Framework (PCF) of the American Productivity & Quality Center (APQC)

Under the Open Standard Benchmarking Collaborative (OSBC), the American Productivity and Quality Center (APQC) has constructed a Process Classification Framework (PCF), as shown in Figure 1, and made it public. Further, APQC announces a revised version every year. APQC explains that the operations of each organization can be understood by PCF from a horizontal process view and not a vertical, functional process view. In PCF, the process hierarchy is classified into four steps — the category, process group, process, and activity. Further, the process hierarchy is coded. For example, "4.0 Deliver Products and Services" in Figure 1 is deployed as illustrated in Figure 2.

## 6  Process Management Unit and Operation Flow

In process management, the process initiated by the event will be described as a management unit on the basis of the partitions of the connected function and activity. In other words, it is necessary to solve the issue of how to

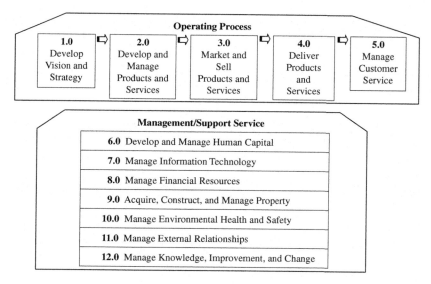

Fig. 1   Process Classification Framework.

*Source*: Ver.5.0.3, April 2008.

(http://www.apqc.org/portal/apqc/site/?path= /research/bmm/osbc/index.html)

4.0   Deliver Products and Services (Category)
4.1   Plan for and acquire necessary resources: Supply Chain Planning
      (Process Group)
4.1.1   Develop production and materials strategies (Process)
4.1.1.1   Define manufacturing goals (Activity)
4.1.1.2   Define labor and materials policies (Activity)

Fig. 2   Example of PCF.

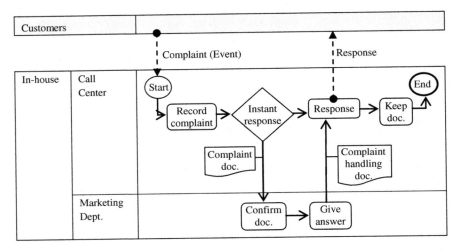

Fig. 3   Example of a Trouble-shooting Process.

*Source*: Takeyasu K. *et al.*, 2007, p. 3; modified by author.
*Note*: "doc." refers to document.

describe and define the process as a management unit. The process management unit is an inter-departmental specific process wherein the output is
repeatedly delivered from the flow of activities connected to two or more
departments. The event is the occurrence that *starts* the process. Therefore,
the event differs from the function that uses *time*. Further, as shown in
Figure 3, the event is related to a point in time. The process *controls* the
functions, in the sense that it is the process that uses a function or the connected functions as a set of activities (Seidelmeier, 2004, pp. 70–71).

Davenport (1993, p. 28) explains the basis for the decision about the
length of the process as follows:

The objective of process identification is the key to making these
definitions and determining their implications. If the objective is

incremental improvement, it is sufficient to work with many narrowly defined processes, as the risk of failure is relatively low. But when the objective is radical process change, a process must be defined as broadly as possible.

Davenport (1993, p. 31) also adds that process definition is more of an art than science.

# 7   Structure of BPM

BPM is "the control and management of transactions between organizations both inside and outside corporations by viewing the transaction flows as processes, which is enabled by breaking up the traditional walls between organizations, sharing information and resources among them, and combining and connecting their transactions". This paper divides BPM into two: a *process chain management* inside the corporation that surpasses the functional and departmental barriers and a *process net strategy* outside the corporation that surpasses the barriers among corporations.

## 7.1   *Process chain management*

In an organization that focuses on functions, the business operation is managed based on the function, and managers naturally consume and manage resources according to the functional budget and emphasize the strict adaptation of standards. Consequently, because employees are eager to observe the functional standards and save resources, the relationships among business process, suppliers, and customers are not optimized (Department of Defense, 1994). Gradually, there emerges an expectation that process chain management will remove the barriers among the functions as shown in Figure 4, to optimize the whole value chain by completing link A, and integrate the main process with the support process by completing link B. IT innovation enhances the possibility of this action.

On the other hand, it is said that in today's competitive environment, a large company does not defeat a smaller one but a fast company defeats a slower one.

However, under the uncertain environment that cannot respond to with a speed alone, there is a demand for a process management system that

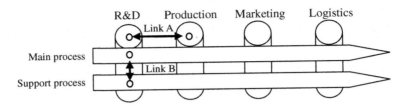

Fig. 4  Value-chain Optimization of Business Process.

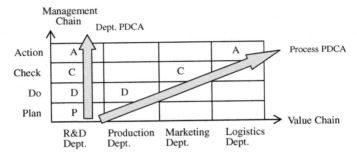

Fig. 5  Value-chain and Process PDCA.

*Note*: "Dept." refers to department.

can manage the process promptly and flexibly according to the changes in the market environment. For such a process management system, it is necessary to achieve a balance between the *value chain* (to manage the process in a horizontal organization) and *management chain* (to manage the horizontal organization using the Plan-Do-Check-Action (PDCA) cycle).

In other words, the process PDCA cycle, rather than the departmental PDCA cycle that occurs within the department, is preferable for the systematic, integrated, continuous improvement of the whole process — this is shown in Figure 5. That is, the management system is expected to perform the process PDCA cycle for all the processes across all departments. As a result, the process PDCA cycle in process chain management is important, as it can improve productivity and corporate value.

In a Balanced Scorecard (BSC), the strategic goal is deployed up to the performance-evaluating indicators of operations. However, the perceptions of the manager or the process manager concerning the performance

measurements are different when the measurement criterion of the operations is not linked with the strategy or when the criterion is not integrated
through the management units of the function and the process, and so forth.
As a result, it is easy to execute a strategy that is not accepted by the
workers in the field. Kittredge (2004) insists that such problems can be
solved if the performance indicators conform to the measurement indicators of the strategically and tactically important processes chosen by the
process managers are reflected in the BSC and these indicators are
deployed on the BSC.

In BSC, the lead indicators are the performance drivers and lag indicators are the outcomes. The *lag indicator* only identifies the present
position, and illustrates the change in the indicator. However, the *lead
indicator* identifies the destination and requires an early decision.
Therefore, we can say that the lead indicator is preferable in process management when it comes to the real-time management of the performance.

In general, the effect of the change in the process on the consump-
tion of resources in the process can be easily identified; however,
estimating the reverse is not that easy. If performance management and
process management harmonize in the manner mentioned above, the
process can be managed by using the performance chain as shown in
Figure 6. In other words, important performance drivers that yield the
desired outcome in BSC can be systemically linked with the strategic
goal if they are chosen from each of the process outputs. In addition,
in BSC, we can also determine the direction of the process management.

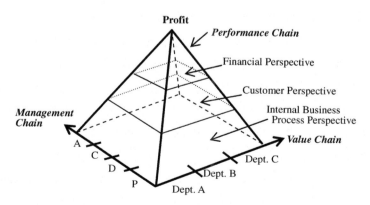

Fig. 6   Integration of the Three Chains.

As a result, at the process level, the targets determined using a top-down approach match the management indicators chosen using the bottom-up approach, and the application of PDCA cycle on BSC becomes possible, such that an integrated management system, as depicted in Figure 6, can be constructed.

## 7.2 *Process net strategy*

The competitive environment has already shifted from competition among companies to competition among process networks that aim to construct a syndicate. In such an environment, the selection, concentration, and collaboration strategies of the process, such as inter-firm process-level alliances, shared services, and outsourcing part of the business process, are adopted because of the expectation that these steps will yield competitive advantage. It is said that the strategic process net construction can be divided into the four following strategies (Yamada and Uchida, 1999).

1. Choose and manage only the function that becomes the key of the competitive advantage within the existing value chain and outsource with the rest to realize lower costs.
2. Aim toward creating an oligopoly in particular processes by focusing on special processes within the existing value chain that add significant value, and supplying the same to multiple companies.
3. Streamline the value chain by cutting the unnecessary processes, and focus on customer-satisfaction.
4. Add value by adding new functions when the customers' needs exceed the capability of the existing value chain.

In other words, the process net strategy is a decision-making approach whereby the processes are selected and concentrated on the basis of the corporate strategy as well as considering the plausible changes in the environment. This approach is adopted both inside and outside the company/country.

Using a strategy that secures the functional advantage in the value chain under a competitive environment, the company is confronted with a decision-making problem — of whether to buy the functional advantage or develop it. In general, in an industry where environmental changes are not that intense, it is preferable for the company to choose the strategy of developing the functional advantage so as to always sustain the mainspring of long-term growth. However, when long-term growth is somewhat elusive, this strategy has a negative effect in that it increases costs. Consequently, the strategy of buying the functional advantage needs to be constructed by the *collaboration of the business process* such as the selection, the concentration, and the collaboration of the business process.

### 7.2.1   *Business process collaboration*

In today's competitive environment, which is characterized by increasing uncertainty and severity, it is necessary to decrease the risk generated by environmental changes and adopt strategic means to maintain and expand one's competitive advantage. In other words, it is necessary to invest limited managerial resources to identify and foster a process that may become a core competence, and to utilize resources outside the corporation, if necessary, for processes other than core competence. This approach is deemed feasible because using other corporations' assets, rather than creating or buying new assets necessary to respond to environmental changes, can decrease the economic risk, and also because this improves corporate flexibility and enables the company to respond to environmental changes in a short amount of time. However, this approach does necessitate that an intra-corporate process network that smoothly connects processes across multiple corporations and that exchanges real-time information regarding the same is built. As this problem is, to a great extent, solvable using the Internet, and in particular, the Web services architecture, such business process networks are possible. Therefore, in the information era, it is said that the company that shares information attains more success than the company that manages information. Figure 7 depicts a case wherein the product is procured from an Electronics Manufacturing Services (EMS) company, i.e., outsourcing, and the data processing is delegated to a special company, i.e., shared service.

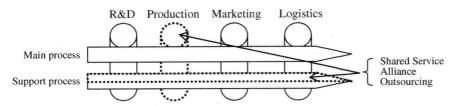

Fig. 7   Business Process Collaboration.

## 7.2.2 *Patterns of business process collaboration*

Alliance, outsourcing, and shared service, and so forth are considered as the main examples of business process collaboration. However, it is not easy to define business process collaboration because the abovementioned features and their ranges can be changed. Therefore, the study proposes that the collaboration is considered to have taken place when the company performs the following activities in the business process network across companies.

Outsourcing: Some particular processes except the processes that the company performs are delegated to another company (or other companies).

Shared service: Similar processes that the companies perform are concentrated together.

Alliance: Some processes that the company performs are supplemented by the cooperating company.

In the IT industry, the system of cheaply procuring components from third parties and assembling them in-house is being generalized. However, there also exist companies that have adopted a reverse strategy and have extended their profits. In the case of Japan, an excellent example would be Matsushita Electric Industrial Co., Ltd., which consistently records high profits as a result of adopting the strategy of "in-house production using vertical integration", where the company consistently handles everything from the components to finished goods. The plasma television production line of the Matsushita Electric Industrial Co., Ltd. is a good example. The following are the advantages of in-house procurement. It is said that the inner procurement rates of the components used in Matsushita's plasma televisions have increased by 50% (Nihon Keizai Shinbun, 2006).

1. In-house production stabilizes the product price by preventing the outsourcing of key components that have a valuable function.
2. Mass production of components results in an increase in the sales volume via external sales of components and this results in a cost reduction of both the components and the product.
3. Incorporating design changes and new technologies in the product while maintaining sales of the product in the global market are easy.

On the other hand, Apple Co., the maker of *iPhone*, while causing a sensation in 2007, adopted a strategy that differs from that adopted by Matsushita. The company uses the capability of component suppliers, spread all over the world, to think what about the customers want and what the maker must do. Apple's case is comparable to the strategy of vertical integration adopted by the Japanese company Matsushita (Nihon Keizai Shinbun, 2007).

## 8  Conclusion

While many new process management techniques have been proposed recently, BPM is the general term used to refer to these. However, process-oriented management is not a new concept in business management; in fact, process-oriented management was simply not feasible until now. Today, cooperation and integration among business processes, which hitherto were impossible, have become possible because data processing and telecommunication have evolved a great deal due to advancements in IT. On the other hand, process management is also required to effectively respond to the changes in the highly competitive environment not only with respect to customer satisfaction but also with time, flexibility, and cost.

Though many companies have attempted process restructuring (e.g., BPR), few have achieved their objectives. It seems that this might be the case because these companies did not establish a process management mechanism to improve the efficiency of the entire process and ensure the stability of the reformed processes, which are the problems of BPR that were mentioned in this study. Hence, while many new process management techniques to overcome such problems are being proposed today, it is not easy to create a systematical method of process management to improve the efficiency and stability of the restructured process.

In the current environment, where the changes are intense and unforeseeable and any past success or experience has lost its meaning, BPM, which allows the synchronization of the company's output with the changes in the environment, will be an effectual tool to obtain competitive advantage.

## References

Daly, C. and T. Freeman. (1997). *The Road of to Excellence: Becoming a Process-Based Company (The CAM-I Process Management Guide)*, Institute of Management Accountants, CAM-I.

Davenport, T.H. (1993). *Process Innovation — Reengineering Work Through Information Technology*, Harvard Business School Press.

Department of Defense. (1994). www.c3i.osd.mil/bpr/bprcd/mhome.htm.

Hammer, M. (July–August 1990). Reengineering Work: Don't Automate, Obliterate, *Harvard Business Review*, pp. 104–112.

Jeston, J. and J. Nelis. (2006). *Business Process Management-Practical Guidelines to Successful Implementations*, Elsevier.

Kittredge, J. (Sep/Oct 2004). Process Management and Cost Management: Collaboration or Opposition, *Cost Management*, pp. 23–30.

Monden, Y. *et al.* (2007). *Japanese Management Accounting Today*, World Scientific.

Nihon Keizai Shinbun (2006). 27 July. (In Japanese)

Nihon Keizai Shinbun (2007). 27 August. (In Japanese)

Seidelmeier, H. (2004). *Business Process Modeling by ARIS*, BNN. (In Japanese)

Smith, H. and P. Finger. (2007). *Business Process Management: The Third Wave*, Meghan-Kiffer Press.

Statements on Management Accounting No. 4NN. (April 2000). *Implementing Process Management for Improving Products and Services*, Institute of Management Accountants.

Takeyasu, K., Miyazaki, Y. and Y. Higuchi. (2007). *The Recording Method of Work Flow for Internal Control*, Chuokeizaisya. (In Japanese)

Yamada, H. and K. Uchida. (1999). Creative Destruction of Value Chain, 10 May, *Nihon Keizai Shinbun*. (In Japanese)

# 2

# Organic Coupling Between BPM and Management Information

Ryuta Uematsu
*Representative, Opt. u., Japan*

This study aims at accomplishing the following ideas in practical business: by connecting BPM and actual cost accounting based on ABC with the latest information technology, controlling timely the operation of the field and cost-accounting for financial accounting; and, at the same time, verifying cost per variety and management indicators in order to determine profitable products.

Moreover, not limited to such a "financial viewpoints", it will also discuss the risk indicators captured by "customers' viewpoint" in the case of failure in process management in the era of enlarged customer power.

## 1  Post-War Development of Japanese Economy

### 1.1  *From post-war high economic growth to medium growth*

Japanese economy had once enjoyed high growth at the year-on-year rate of nine percent on average continuously for 17 years from 1955 to 1973. Because heavy industries led this era with seniority-based pay scale system and lifetime employment, the Japanese could believe in continuous enhancement of the quality of life. However, the first oil shock in 1973 saw the Japanese economic growth rate decline year after year since then. This event guided Japanese economy to the era of medium growth.

### 1.2  *To mature economy through the bubble economy*

For the next 17 years from 1974 to 1991, Japanese economy had enjoyed medium-rate economic growth at the year-on-year rate of four percent on average. For those years, Japanese economy had still possessed vitality. Main industries moved to automobile, consumer-electronics, and computer.

Personal computers also emerged and spread widely during this period. On the other hand, the appreciation of the yen triggered by the Plaza Accord engendered the age of historically low interest rate and bubble economy, which finally left much destruction on Japanese economy.

Then, from 1992 to 2007, the year-on-year growth rate of Japanese economy had long stayed only at one percent on average, including the year of negative growth. Japanese businesses have promoted overseas transfer of production, not only to Southeast Asia, Europe and the United States but also to China since the 1990s. Relating to the improvement of personal computers, the significant advance of software has made it accessible to people to process given information, and the spread of the Internet has provided many choices of information to users. Meanwhile, the maturity of economy has accelerated irregular employment. Japanese economy has faced such a phase that requires the transformation of industrial structure or new industry creation which revitalizes nationals as well as new management methods which strengthen business vitality.

Other aspects of history of the post-war Japanese economy are: the structural change from "low-mix/high-volume/large-size" in the era of high economic growth to the "high-mix/low-volume/small-size" in the era of mature economy; enlargement of customer power in the era of mature economy because of excess-supply; and the wide-range and free acquisition of information by the highly improved technology of the Internet.

## 2  Utility and Limit of ERP

Since the 1990s, Japan has entered into the era of mature economy. In the realm of computer hardware, personal computer diffused together with promotion of downsizing. Meanwhile, in the realm of computer software, many kinds of software packages such as ERP, SCM, PDM, CRM, and SFA have been introduced by Western countries. Among these software packages, ERP for mission-critical tasks has commanded the most attention among businesses in Japan.

ERP is a supporting tool which allocates management resources efficiently to the whole company. The two most important advantages are company-wide unified data management and real-time data updates. In Japanese businesses, there have been pros and cons of the introduction of this software package, and several companies still have a resistance to ERP. The typical reason of the resistance is that the business process provided by ERP is unsuitable for the workflow of the company.

Evaluations of ERP should be organized as follows:

(1) Mission-critical task means the basic workflow of business processing such as order entry, purchase, production, shipment, acceptance inspection, billing, collection of bill, accounting, and closing of accounts. In this workflow, the part which the enterprise can differentiate other companies is chiefly production management. As other parts have few factors to differentiate others, there is no merit to fixate own company's original workflow. In an extreme instance, conformity to the rule of ERP must be the best way. In other words, it is the least expensive way of business processing and paperwork cost.

(2) The next is the sphere which mission-critical tasks do not cover. First of all, the functions mentioned above do not include cost accounting. Even if ERP has the function of cost accounting, it is often inadequate for companies to survive in the era of mature economy. Although cost accounting is an essential element for both financial accounting and management accounting, it is highly difficult to provide the capability of cost accounting for both of them. The poor performance of cost accounting of ERP would fail to offer management information such as profit performance per variety or per customer and the analysis of profit variance between budget and actual profit.

(3) While business process will be streamlined by ERP, it does not equip the function of monitoring the efficiency of one simple process or the quantity of inter-process stocks, figuring out the reality of the operation in the field in real time. Accordingly, albeit outfitting the function of recording the acceptance and withdrawal on quantity and the amount of dealing, ERP lacks the function of figuring out the actual condition of business process or of recording the acceptance and withdrawal time of quantity. If these features are required, another means must be arranged.

# 3   Cost of Sales and Cost Accounting of Financial Accounting, and the Relation with Management Accounting

## 3.1   *Utility and limit of standard cost accounting*

Standard cost accounting takes the following steps in the budget-making process: firstly, assessing unit cost, yield and others of variable cost per process and per variety including material cost; secondly, and similarly, assessing fixed cost per process by considering productivity of each variety; finally, formulating overhead cost based on specific rules.

Therefore, the following formula will be approved:

$\sum$ (standard cost per variety × budgetary quantity per variety) = budgetary incurred cost per account classification.

Since actual quantity must be multiplied by standard cost in the case of assessing actual cost, the following formula will be approved:

$\sum$ (standard cost per variety × actual quantity per variety) + cost variance = actual cost per account classification.

Among these elements, standard cost per variety, actual quantity per variety and actual cost per account classification have the clear-cut breakdown or the basis for calculation. Accordingly, the effectiveness of standard cost accounting system hinges on the lucidness of cost variance.

(1) Small amount of cost variance: if actual cost approximated to budgetary cost, variance cost would be a small amount. In this case, it is not necessary to analyze the variance cost. Such situations tend to happen in the era of high economic growth.

(2) Large amount of cost variance — case 1: if actual sales-size is differentiated from budgetary one with little change in product configuration from budget, variance cost would be explained by "utilization variance", which is generally assessed by simple arithmetic. Hence, a standard cost system functions effectively in this case.

(3) Large amount of cost variance — case 2: if actual sales-size is differentiated from budgetary one with substantial change of variety configuration from budget, it would be difficult to survive with a standard cost system. That is because not only utilization variance has to be traced, variance of product configuration also has to be traced in order to figure out cost variance. This tracing work would be as arduous task as the tasks of standard cost-accounting per process and per variety in the budget-making algorithm. Furthermore, if full-scale trace was required, it would be an impossible task including the substituting of the estimate value of production efficiency with the actual value.

In the era of high economic growth, when planned and expected performance was achieved, standard cost system had some utilities such as a model as budgetary cost per process and per variety, conciseness and quickness of calculating the actual cost and understandability of comparison of budget and actual. However, in the era of mature economy characterized by "high-mix/low-volume", quick market change, and repeated adjacent order change from customers, variety configuration change occurs frequently. That is why standard cost accounting is becoming insufficient in this era.

## 3.2 *Function and performance of cost accounting in the sight of management accounting*

Businesses which do not have difficulties ensuring sufficient sales-size have little incentive to focus on cost accounting. Those kinds of businesses are required to only cost-account on the rule of financial accounting. In other words, they should be only able to distinguish between the cost required to be included in current period and the same in the next one, and it is no problem if the costing is rational and valid in the viewpoint of financial accounting and tax practice. It scarcely becomes an issue whether any cost accounting function in the field of management accounting.

However, few companies achieve sufficient sales-size easily, and acquiring profit involves many difficulties. For this reason, companies cannot help but pay inevitable attention to cost. At that time, because cost accounting of financial accounting is insufficient to the end, necessary information should be assured on the standpoint of management accounting. Moreover, that information has to be processed to analyze cost structure.

Next, it is the issue of consistency of cost accounting between financial accounting and management accounting. If there was no consistency between them, the accomplishment of cost reformation based on the indicator by management accounting would not reflect the financial accounting when companies balance the book. The requirement of cost accounting is interlocking among manufacturing management indicator, management accounting indicator, and financial accounting indicator. Figure 1 illustrates this relationship. According to this figure, cost accounting is the interface to interlock between financial accounting and management accounting.

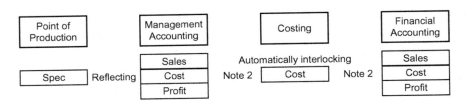

Fig. 1   Relationship Among 3 Indicators.

*Note* 1: Sales amount is automatically interlocked between financial accounting and management accounting.

*Note* 2: Cost must be artificially interlocked between financial accounting and management accounting.

## 4   Characteristics of Mature Economy and Economical Evaluation

As mentioned in the last portion of Section 1, one of the characteristics of the mature economy is "high-mix/low-volume". In contrast to "low-mix/high-volume" of the high economic growth, it is difficult to construct the effectively functioning scheme of management accounting unless the impact of "high-mix/low-volume" to productivity or cost structure is clarified.

### 4.1   *Economic performance indicator required by "high-mix/low volume"*

#### 4.1.1   *Price is high, but cost is higher?*

Because of the diversified customer orientation and transfer of the production of low grade items to Southeast Asia and China, the production in Japan tends to specialize in high grade items. Diversification and high-grade is promoting further "high-mix/low-volume".

Although cost-conscious industries have taken measures to "high-mix/low-volume", not all companies have been able to accomplish that. If measures to incorporate "high-mix/low-volume" including the thoroughness of target costing and offline setup were insufficient in new industries, they would fail to grow because of malfunction of the management. If mature economy went into this situation, economic stagnation would be fixed.

In addition, if no cost information is given to sales department, according to Japanese traditional culture, sales people may misunderstand that high-grade and high-price products are more profitable than low-grade and low-price ones". That is to say, the more they sell, the more they lose.

Thus, in the case of "high-mix/low-volume/high grade products", the cost might be more expensive than people suppose. To confirm this, there is no way but to construct the scheme which can verify cost structure in great detail.

### 4.1.2   *Inhibitory element on fixed cost productivity*

Production volume per unit fixed cost should be higher. For this purpose, it is ideal to keep producing varieties which can be produced efficiently. Practically, there are also orders of inefficient production, of high-mix, and of low-volume. Generally speaking, the smaller the size, the more varieties, and the lower mix the order is, the lower the productivity is.

Given the trend of high-mix and low-volume, measures should be taken to shorten the time of mold exchange by offline setup. However, there are also problems which cannot be prevented in advance, such as the cleansing of the line.

It is a familiar story that an order from a customer is changed at the last minute of production because of the rapid change of the market. The risk of declining the productivity would increase by being disturbing the production schedule.

The waning productivity per unit fixed cost deteriorates corporate performance. In addition, since decrease in productivity increases fixed cost per product, it lessens the profit per product. In this manner, additional attention is required to assure the productivity per unit fixed cost.

Note: Even if productivity per unit fixed cost increases, low price products cannot earn a large amount of profit. To enlarge the profit in the short run, it is required to be considered both unit marginal profit per variety and productivity. However, in the case which there is no choice of order, realistic approach would be improving the productivity in order of priority. Ideal theory is expressed by following formulae:

Marginal profit per hour [yen/hour] =
$\Sigma$ (unit marginal profit per variety [yen/unit] × productivity per variety [unit/hour])
Amount of profit = production by order of priority of marginal profit per hour per variety.

## 4.2 *Impact on business caused by unforeseen event*

### 4.2.1 *Characteristics of customer behavior in the age of continuous excess-supply*

In mature economies, supply is basically the state of excess. In the era of high economic growth, suppliers could decide the delivery date when customers bought desired products. Though this situation could happen locally now, it is basically still a buyer's market. Suppliers are committed in increasing customer satisfaction by shortening the delivery time.

Another characteristic of customer behavior is order change in the last minute of production. This is affected by the environment which customers are also forced to change orders because of market change. This is influenced highly by the condition of buyer's market.

### 4.2.2 *Impact on business management caused by inter-process stocks*

For producers, there are double burdens of shortened delivery date and frequent order change. In that situation, adjacent order change disrupts the order of production process even if an ideal production plan is constructed. It would bring about a non-operating state in the production process because of material deficiency, or produce inter-process stock.

There are three ideas on how to handle these situations with sufficient stock:

(1) According to the mind-set in the era of high economic growth, internal interest expense on stocks should be considered. Because it indeed accrues in financial accounting, it should also be calculated in management account.
(2) According to the mind-set in the era of medium economic growth, the influence of stock reduction activities should be considered. While internal interest expense on stocks accrues by possessing stocks, the order would be canceled by missing the delivery time under stock reduction activity. In this case, even if internal interest expense on stocks does not accrue, the evaluation should be opportunity loss and the loss of marginal profit for the order.
(3) How should it be evaluated according to the mind-set in the era of mature economy? The order would be lost by missing the delivery

time in the same way as (2), its impact would not remain in losing the order because of supply-excess. Not only are there many other suppliers, but also their information is easily obtained on the internet. Hence, it should be recognized that suppliers could lose the customer as well as the order.

### 4.3    *Historically sophisticated management and the object of management accounting*

As mentioned, the characteristics of a market changes with time, and this change influences the managing condition of the company. Hence, management accounting must change to adapt it. Management accounting should be understood more than just the unraveling of the actual profit structure of the enterprise or the analyzing of the variance from budget. It should assume the role of evaluating risk in the future.

## 5    Process Management and Economic Performance Indicator

### 5.1    *Single process management and time related information*

#### 5.1.1    *Single process management for cost reduction and improvement of fixed cost productivity*

Post-war Japanese manufacturing business of production model had the history of improving productivity and reducing cost. In the process of productivity improvement in assembly line, the goal was set to each process, and day-to-day amelioration was repeated. Although this mass production method by assembly line tends to be replaced by sell production system, the goal, in any case, is the improvement of productivity. Advanced manufacturing business of production model almost finished the pursuance of efficiency of single unit. It is said that productivity improvement cannot be expected any more.

In the case of single process, the better the productivity is, the lesser the unit fixed cost is. For that reason, process occupation time needs to be recorded per variety. Alternatively, amount of time required to complete an operation. By utilizing the information of amount time to estimate fixed cost per variety, cost accounting can reflect the actual realities.

### 5.1.2   *Inter-process management: upholding the efficiency between processes*

If the production was not as scheduled at certain process because of order change of customer or some troubles, there would be problems in the vicinity. Before that process, pretreatment stock would accumulate. The next process would be non-operating state because the materials would not arrive. Thus, the disordered flow between processes deteriorates the whole production capacity. Whereas it can be restrained with prevention of order change and trouble in production, it is realistically impossible. Therefore, the important countermeasures are minimizing the influence of occurred disordered flow and fixing it to the normal.

In the past, veterans in the production control department took charge on that sort of work with experimental knowledge. However, recently, supporting tools of designing smooth flow between processes has been developed because of development of information technologies.

### 5.1.3   *Fixed cost productivity indicator and fixed cost accounting*

Then, productivity indicator of single process and inter-process should be considered. The following four requirements should be covered:

1.  Elements determining productivity should be decomposed;
2.  Decomposed elements should have each meaning;
3.  Decomposed elements should be mutually exclusive and collectively exhaustive; and
4.  The improvement of productivity should be reflected rationally to cost accounting.

Satisfying these requirements is the condition of indicator accepted by all members.

Figure 2 expresses an indicator of productivity per fixed cost for manufacturing business of production model. (i) This productivity indicator is decomposed into four elements of capacity utilization ratio, production efficiency (quantity of processing per hour), yield, and fixed cost per month (time rate). (ii) Each element has a meaning. (iii) Product of these four elements is quantity of non-defective products per unit fixed cost. However, generally, the better the production efficiency is, the worse the

| Time related information | Monthly hours $H_M$ | | | |
|---|---|---|---|---|
| | Utilized hours $H_S + H_L$ | | | Unutilized hours |
| | Occupied hours by Non-defective products $H_S$ | | Occupied hours by Defective products $H_L$ | |
| Yield Quantity | Non-defective quantity $Q_S$ | | Defective quantity $Q_L$ | |
| | Material input quantity $Q_S + Q_L$ | | | |
| Cost | Monthly fixed cost $FC$ | | | |

$$\frac{Q_S}{FC} = \frac{H_S + H_L}{H_M} \times \frac{Q_S + Q_L}{H_S + H_L} \times \frac{Q_S}{Q_S + Q_L} \times \frac{H_M}{FC}$$

| PuFC | Utilization | Efficiency | Yield | Fixed Cost |
|---|---|---|---|---|

Fig. 2　Productivity Per Unit Fixed Cost: PuFC.

Fixed cost per non-detective product: FCNP

$$\frac{Q_S}{FC} = \frac{H_S + H_L}{H_M} \times \frac{Q_S + Q_L}{H_S + H_L} \times \frac{Q_S}{Q_S + Q_L} \times \frac{H_M}{FC}$$

| PuFC | Utilization | Efficiency | Yield | Fixed Cost |
|---|---|---|---|---|

**Consistently-formulated between upper and lower equation.**

$$\frac{FC}{Q_S} = \frac{H_M}{H_S + H_L} \times \frac{H_S + H_L}{Q_S + Q_L} \times \frac{Q_S + Q_L}{Q_S} \times \frac{FC}{H_M}$$

| FCNP | Utilization | Efficiency | Yield | Fixed Cost |
|---|---|---|---|---|

Fig. 3　Fixed Cost Per Non-Detective Product: FCNP.

yield is. That is, the relationship between production efficiency and yield is trade-off. In addition, because decline of fixed cost per month causes lowering of wages or increase in nonpermanent employees, implementation of it needs many challenges and difficulties.

Next, the lower formula in Figure 3 is one reversed numerator and denominator of Figure 2. In this formula, the left-hand side expresses fixed cost per non-defective product. Consequently, increase and decrease of productivity steadily reflect in fixed cost accounting.

As a whole, this section can be summarized in following points:

• Figure 2

1. The higher the capacity utilization ratio is, the higher the productivity per fixed cost is.
2. The higher the production efficiency is, the higher the productivity per fixed cost is.
3. The higher the yield is, the higher the productivity per fixed cost is.
4. The lower the fixed cost per month, the higher the productivity per fixed cost is.

• Figure 3

1. The higher the capacity utilization ratio is, the lower the fixed cost per non-defective product is.
2. The higher the production efficiency is, the lower the fixed cost per non-defective product is.
3. The higher the yield is, the lower the fixed cost per non-defective product is.
4. The lower the fixed cost per month, the lower the fixed cost per non-defective product is.

Note: the explanation above is the example of process type manufacturing business. In the case of assembly type, quantity of processing per hour of the second term in the formulae should be amount of hours per processing. The basic structure of the formulae for both types is the same except reversing numerator and denominator.

### 5.1.4  *Analysis of variation of four elements of fixed cost productivity from budget*

Fixed cost productivity and fixed cost per non-defective product also have budget and actual. Inevitably, there is a variation between budget and actual. The variation should be explained as explained below.

There are three requirements:

(i) It should clarify impact of each element.
(ii) Weight of the impact should be expressed in the format of money.
(iii) Sum of the prices of impact should be equal to the variance between budget and actual.

To satisfy these requirements, indicators should be decomposed in the way showed in Figure 4. In this figure, "A" and "a" are capacity utilization ratio, "B" and "b" are production efficiency, "C" and "c" are yield, and "D" and "d" are fixed cost per month. In addition, capital letters are budgeted value, and small ones are actual value.

## 5.2 *Inter-process management and profit information*

This section tries to construct the model of measuring customer loss risk in the case of failing process management in mature economy.

### 5.2.1 *Impact of customer loss*

Figure 5 is the model of the case which the enterprise of annual sales of one billion loses a middle-ranking customer. Although there is no guarantee of succeeding process management of business with paramount customer, this model presumes failure in business with a middle-ranking customer which accounts for 3.6% of sales. It is supposed that delivery delay for total order of certain month occurs $(3.6\% \div 12 = 0.3\%)$. In addition, it is also supposed that opportunity loss of this case equals marginal profit. If order from this customer is placed again after next month, the effect remains only as the opportunity loss.

In a contrasting situation, the loss of customer which stops its order after next month is eternal opportunity loss.

Actual

$$\text{Budget} : \alpha = A \times B \times C \times D$$

$$\text{Actual} : \beta = a \times b \times c \times d$$

$$
\begin{aligned}
&\text{Actual} : \beta \;-\; \text{Budget} : \alpha \\
=\;& abcd \;-\; ABCD \\
=\;& (a-A)BCD \;+\; a(b-B)CD \;+\; ab(c-C)D \;+\; abc(d-D)
\end{aligned}
$$

| Variance of Utilization | Variance of Efficiency | Variance of Yield | Variance of Fixed Cost |
|:---:|:---:|:---:|:---:|
| ↑ | ↑ | ↑ | ↑ |
| Single Factor | Single Factor | Single Factor | Single Factor |

Fig. 4   Variance Analysis Between Budget and Actual.

**Original Status**      **One Month's Loss**     ← **Middle Ranking Customer of 3.6% Share**

| Annual | Base Profit | | Opportunity Loss 0.3% | After Opportunity Loss | | Customer Loss 3.6% | After Costomer Loss |
|---|---|---|---|---|---|---|---|
| Sales | 1,000,000 | 100% | -3,000 | 997,000 | | -36,000 | 964,000 |
| Valiable | 500,000 | 50% | -1,500 | 498,500 | | -18,000 | 482,000 |
| Fixed | 250,000 | 25% | | 250,000 | | | 250,000 |
| Manu. Cost | 750,000 | 75% | -1,500 | 748,500 | | -18,000 | 732,000 |
| Gross Profit | 250,000 | 25% | -1,500 | 248,500 | | -18,000 | 232,000 |
| Valiable | 30,000 | 3% | -90 | 29,910 | | -1,080 | 28,920 |
| Fixed | 100,000 | 10% | | 100,000 | | | 100,000 |
| Sales Cost | 130,000 | 13% | -90 | 129,910 | | -1,080 | 128,920 |
| Mng. Cost | 50,000 | 5% | | 50,000 | | | 50,000 |
| Sales Profit | 70,000 / 7.0% | 7% | -1,410 / -0.1% | 68,590 / 6.9% | L | -16,920 / -1.7% | 53,080 / 5.3% |

| | Labour @ | 8,000 | → After a half year | →G | -4,000 |
|---|---|---|---|---|---|
| Sales Cost | Num. of Per. | 10 | aquire a new customer | | |
| | Labour C | 80,000 | Recovering of a half year | R | 8,460 L×6/12 |

**Impact**     L + G + R    -12,460    -1.246%

Less Significant Impact of Opportunity Loss    In case of 6 Customers Loss, Sales Profit goes to the Red

Fig. 5    Production Trouble Simulation.

### 5.2.2 Operating expense for acquisition of alternative new customer

However, the eternal opportunity loss could be stopped by acquiring a new customer with marketing efforts. Trial calculation of the case of taking half a year for getting new customer is showed in the Figure 5. Realistically, there is a possibility of spread of customer loss information in the industry, and the term of six months would not be sufficient to gain new customers. Considering this, the calculation should be said to express the case of minimum effect of customer loss.

### 5.3 From the age of exclusive management indicator to that of open management indicator

The evaluation for inter-process stock remained in the financial sphere as the internal interest expense on stocks. However, customer power has been enlarged with the state of excess-supply today. That is why opportunity loss with customer loss or sales cost for acquiring new customers should be recognized as risk. In this way, risk has to be considered with "customer viewpoint" as well as "financial viewpoint".

## Summary

In some foreign countries, the era of BPM has already begun. In Japan, it should be necessary for companies facing the risk of customer loss to introduce BPM. At the same time, using the time regarded information which is obtained as byproduct, it is possible to apply that information to actual costing. Moreover, the scheme of analysis of the variance between budget and actual became enabled through dividing both productivity per variety and cost accounting into four factors.

# 3

# The Business Process Network Strategy of SMEs

Satoshi Arimoto
*Niigata University, Japan*

## 1  Introduction

In recent years, the small and medium-sized enterprises (SMEs) that make up an important segment of Japan's manufacturing industry and have been a source of its competitive strength have been exposed to a harsh business environment. Some causes are the soaring price of crude oil and other raw materials — the same economic environment that big businesses face. Other causes are a variety of structural factors specific to SMEs, such as the decline of so-called *keiretsu* transactions. As a result, SMEs are losing the backing of manufacturers. The stress of these domestic and international pressures has been compounded as they came pouring in at the same time. In such an economic environment, Japan's economy has recovered since the collapse of the bubble economy and the so-called lost decade of stagnation. However, the recoveries of the SMEs delay, and the larger number of corporate bankruptcies of SMEs have continued.

In this economic environment, SMEs are seeking new ways of survival. It goes without saying that they must enhance their competitiveness through their own effort and initiative. In addition, however, SMEs are trying to strengthen links with other companies to build networks of collaboration. This paper presents an overview of the current situation and challenges of an SME network, exploring the network as a business process, and analyzing the significance of managing the SMEs' business processes within such a network.

## 2  Change Required for SMEs

Existing SMEs, like any company large or small, are currently required to rapidly respond to changes in the economic environment. First of all, product life cycles have been shrinking for a long time, which means that SMEs face considerable pressure in adhering to a short delivery time. Moreover, due to the diversification of customer preferences, custom-made and small-lot production is in high demand. These factors are causing major changes in Japan's SMEs as the most important source of competitiveness shifts from price (cost) to the ability to respond with speed and flexibility to the economic environment.

Manufacturers make extensive demands to their SME suppliers, beginning with price (cost) cuts, of course. Next, manufacturers gauge their satisfaction with the SMEs by the latter's ability to respond to changes in lead time to protect the delivery cycle. This has made SME owners more aware of the customer satisfaction index. In recent years, the growing concern with customer satisfaction — something difficult to quantify in metrics — is not limited to SMEs. In fact, SMEs owners must pay attention to factors that were not vary important in the era of mass production accompanied by a long life cycle.

In addition to the ability to respond rapidly to changes in the economic environment, changes in the structure of trade have had a significant impact on SMEs.

In a 2007 White Paper on small and medium-sized enterprises in Japan, an increase in mesh transactions was reported (refer Figure 1). The left side of the chart shows the flow of so-called *keiretsu* transactions. Because of the decline in *keiretsu* transactions, SMEs must develop and

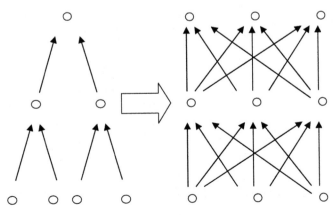

Fig. 1   A Changing "Mesh" of Trade Relations.

*Source*: 2007 White Paper on small and medium-sized enterprises in Japan, p. 158.

maintain a variety of business contacts. The right side of the chart shows mesh transactions. In this White Paper, a growing trend was reported for SMEs to increase the number of trading partners. On one hand, the various customer demands on SMEs are increasing; on the other hand, the number of trading partners is increasing. As a result, the load created by the processing of transactions for SMEs is dramatically heavier.

By adopting, a modular approach, manufacturers now consider core competence as an element of versatility. In addition, manufacturers seek a global partner to raise their versatility. In my opinion, Japan's technology is still at the top level. However, the technical ability of the so-called underdeveloped countries is advancing significantly. Moreover, in terms of cost advantage, these countries have taken the lead. SMEs coming out from under the protective umbrella of *keiretsu* transactions face prodigious global competition.

In the face of a harsh economic situation, many SMEs have developed their own competitiveness in order to establish a strong position in the world. In the 2008 White Paper on SMEs Japan, it was reported that many of them achieved global success by providing high value-added products, and not through mass production or cost advantage.

To survive in this economic climate, the main objective of SMEs is to gain competitiveness of their own and focus on the networking of business processes. For SMEs that manage a single or fractional process, the volume of orders that one SME can manage is limited. Thus, SMEs build collaborative networks, and through network management, try to increase the value-added approach of their own businesses.

## 3   SMEs' Collaboration with Outside Organizations

Now, I shall try to organize the features of SMEs' business processes. First of all, from the view of the final product manufacturers, SMEs manage either a single or fractional process. For them, the important question is how SMEs can contribute to the global optimization required in the production of the final product. SMEs' contribution is usually measured by the price, delivery time and ability to respond to changes in orders. On the other hand, SMEs have the know-how to optimize their own processes, and manage each break-even point. Of course, if SMEs have a high degree of operational capacity in each area, this has an enormous impact when it comes to decision-making to receive additional orders. Moreover, manpower issues are affected by how SMEs secure and maintain employee headcount at the current level of operations. Therefore, maximizing the benefits of SMEs offering linked business processes is the key to the success of the network.

With reference to the SMEs business processes network, it is important to clarify how we should view the network. The business processes of SMEs should be viewed from two dimensions (refer Figure 2). When viewed from downstream of the final product, one dimension is how to align the company's own process with that of the business process directly before or after (horizontal dimension of Figure 2). Not surprisingly, SMEs need to pursue global optimization of the business process and cooperate with upstream and/or downstream firms.

Figure 2 illustrates a simple business process, where there are four processes A to D leading to completion of the final product. SMEs are charged with process B. From the standpoint of alignment with the process immediately before or after, SMEs will be required to make adjustments to coordinate with processes A and C for global optimization. On the other hand, the volume of business processes that one SME can manage is limited. Therefore, three SMEs are charged with process B while cooperating with each other. This is the point of collaboration between SMEs. As shown in Figure 2, several SMEs are in charge of one business process.

On the other hand, only one SME is in charge of a particular business process. However, through SMEs network, the risk of losing other business

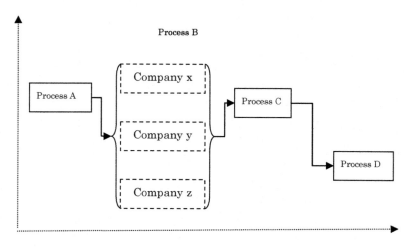

Fig. 2  Two Dimensions of an SME Business Process Network.

opportunities can be reduced. Because one SME is in charge of a particular business process, other SMEs can take another or additional orders. From the manufacturer's viewpoint, alignment with the process before and after is invaluable as it seeks global optimization of its final products. On the other hand, the collaboration between SMEs creates a network that can respond to the most extreme manufacturer demands that, on an individual SME, would normally put a lot of constraints on management. So, this view can be said to be the SMEs' view (vertical dimension of Figure 2).

In this example, three SMEs do the same business process. The same process in several companies that can be done at the same time; however, from an extreme point of view, there are companies that can performs similar process. The essence of the business process network of resource-constrained SMEs is to complement the strengths and weaknesses of each individual company to create opportunities for high value-added business. The final product manufacturers will make a variety of demands, seeing the SME network as one trading partner. High value-added business should have a high degree of customer satisfaction, and requires an advanced ability to respond to changes in the economic environment or to the diversification of customer needs, i.e. in price (cost) or other factors. Thus, it is essential to manage the entire network to improve customer satisfaction.

A problem for the SMEs, however, becomes how to manage each SME's participating network. In other words, how do we measure each SME's contribution when providing high value-added business? This can be defined as internal management.

The SMEs network of business processes does not promise to be as strong a commitment as *keiretsu* ties. SMEs network is also different from businesses that SMEs manage on their own. Rather, SMEs network is in intermediate form of the transaction. While maintaining a loose commitment, it is a challenge for networked SMEs business processes on how to manage the benefits and/or price.

## 4 Current Status and Issues of SMEs' External Cooperation in a Survey in the Niigata Area

In the winter of 2007, we conducted a survey of SMEs in the Niigata area, and asked them how they managed their business processes. Because of the number of samples, statistical hypothesis testing could not be done.

But in this survey, we gained a number of important insights and implications.

## 4.1   *About the competitive environment*

In the current competitive economic environment, many companies believe that price is important, followed by the continued attention to delivery and quality. This means that SMEs are exposed to stiff competition to provide high quality products at low prices, in the current economic environment of shortening product life cycles. On the other hand, the importance of customer satisfaction has been recognized by numerous SMEs. Many SMEs think that it is as necessary to maintain a high level of quality or delivery, as it is to compete on price.

It is very interesting to note that many SMEs think that the ability to develop new products is important. When *Keiretsu* ties were in the mainstream, SMEs were only required to do what the manufacturerers asked for. Currently, SMEs offer manufacturers high value-added products themselves.

## 4.2   *Awareness of external cooperation*

Most companies manage business processes through their own proprietary methods. On the other hand, some SMEs manage any process, e.g. production (manufacturing and assembly) and logistics processes, through commission or joint management. In particular, for the logistics process, there are many cases of cooperation. It is also common for SMEs to contract an external organization that has the experience and expertise in transportation methods. Often, quick deliveries are a sign that an SME cooperating or attempting to cooperate with an outside organization.

On the other hand, in the management of SMEs, there are many concerns when cooperating with an external organization. Many SMEs have pointed out the complexity of management and that SME owners think that cross-organizational management is insignificant with its higher cost. In the survey responses, there is a fewer number of SMEs that worry about the leakage of technology to other companies. This means that complexity of operation and cost are the major hindrances to collaboration with an outside organization. In addition, it is interesting to note that a surplus of labor problems is bigger than imagined.

## 4.3  The future of collaboration with outside organizations

According to the survey results, we can see that many SMEs are interested in cooperating with outside companies in product planning and development and sales processes. Since many SMEs view their product development capacity as the source of future competitiveness, cooperating with an external organization is an important means of achieving this.

In the survey, we also asked about investment in information. Currently, SMEs have only a slight margin for investments in information in collaboration with outside organizations or to build a cooperative network. The cost of participating in the network is a key consideration when setting aside budget for the building of any network. A key factor to be considered while building a network of SMEs is reducing cost barriers to participation in the network, while sharing the benefits of the network to gain future competitiveness. SME networks must have greater competitiveness than the individual business on its own. In addition, unlike *keiretsu* ties that were managed through a capital tie-up, networks should be managed through the moderate method which means that SMEs have a certain degree of independence and rules.

## 5  The Meaning of Building a Business Process Network of SMEs

Many SMEs are aware of the business limitations. On the other hand, we only have to look at the current situation to understand the risk involved in building a business process network of SMEs. From a cost-benefit analysis, SMEs curb information investments or network participation costs, and boost the benefits. This section highlights the significance of building a network.

First, SMEs have a major constraint on management. They receive orders within the constraints of their production capacity, and because of shorter life cycles and the diversification of consumer tastes in recent years, SMEs are required to fine-tune for changes in orders. These factors cause arrangement loss. Compared to production systems for the mass production of small varieties, SMEs are faced with more capacity constraints. Therefore, the significance of building the network is to secure capacity. Through building a network of SMEs that engage in similar business, SMEs can expand their volume of orders.

By securing production capacity, SMEs can expand opportunities for earning revenue from larger orders. And even if one company or several companies in the network have reached their full capacity, the ability to receive extra orders is expected to increase. Therefore, working at full capacity leads to a reduced risk of future loss of earnings. Compared to large companies with large resource constraints, this is likely to be an big advantage.

With the decline in *keiretsu* transactions, SMEs are in a difficult environment to maintain long and stable transactions. As a result, manufacturers have started to screen SMEs. In the White Paper on small and medium-sized enterprises in Japan 2007, it is reported that many SMEs have been increasing the number of their trading partners. If an SME is operating at full capacity and has to decline business opportunities, manufacturers will change trading partners immediately.

In addition, securing production capacity allows fixed costs to be distributed among several companies while securing production scale, i.e. risk dispersion effects can be expected. The distributed effect of this risk also means the distributed risk of bankruptcy for SMEs. The entire network takes responsibility for certain orders. For manufacturers, the risk of outsourcing components or processes to an external organization in a harsh economic environment is reduced. Moreover, this will have a positive effect on credit, which is important for the management of SMEs.

The network of SMEs is significant in securing capacity, but it does not mean that a network is just a patchwork of SMEs engaging in the same business. If several SMEs can be in charge of the same operations, there are other SMEs outside the network which could also take charge of the same operations. If so, there is no positive incentive to order through the network, except for cost factors. To use a hackneyed expression, it is important to get synergy effects from building the network. The network must also show manufacturers what the value-added quotient will be when they place an order with the network.

Another significance of an SME network is to enable manufacturers to distinguish themselves by providing high value-added businesses.

With regards to the flexibility of SMEs, there exists a notion of flexible specialization. By securing a small and flexible expertise through the entire network, we can see the significance of network management. Through this, SMEs can have more flexibility to cope with the uncertain economic environment while maintaining technical expertise. In addition, when several companies are in charge of different business processes, concurrent processes can be managed. This will be a big help when responding to time demands like short delivery schedules. Moreover, when different expertise is needed to deal with a sudden change in orders, it can be expected that flexibility will increase even greater because any number of participating companies can respond.

With regards to manufacturers' use of outside organizations, there is an ongoing debate on a different topics such as outsourcing method. Generally, the underlying concept is that companies should specialize, carrying out only what is necessary from the perspective of their so-called core competence. Of course, this is one way of thinking. But, it is dangerous to say categorically describe. In recent years, in the pursuit of greater professionalism, it has become a widespread idea that companies should use outside organizations in order to build their own core competence. In this situation, SMEs are required to shift from a contract transaction business style to a business style where SMEs actively propose initiatives to the manufacturers for more specialized and high value-added business. The response to this movement is the means of survival for SMEs. Hence, this may be another major significance of building business process network of SMEs. Moreover, as apparent from our previous survey, SMEs place importance on the ability to develop new products for the future source of their competitiveness. By providing the expertise of several companies through the network, SMEs can provide value-added businesses that a single SME cannot provide.

Thus, we can conclude the significance of building an SMEs network below. By building a moderate network that has flexibility, the network has the ability to respond to large size orders. At the same time, by building a network that demonstrates specialized flexibility, the network can provide value-added components to the business. From the perspectives of capacity and discrimination, this is the course to achieving the primary significance, to broaden the scope of an existing business. Furthermore, SME networks will play an important role in creating a business that goes beyond the existing scope of business.

## 6  A Search for Management Methods for Business Process Networks for SMEs

In the current economic environment, building an SMEs network is increasing has gained much importance. How should the network then be managed? For example, SMEs in the same trade/industry tend to congregate in a specific area. From the industrial parks of the cities to rural industrial land, a variety of SME groups have been established. In these areas, prior to the development of IT technology, sharing of tacit knowledge and work practices existed, and the formation of a certain level of network has long been known and utilized. However, many of these are simply at the level of knowledge-sharing. The future network of SME business processes is not simply connections between individual SMEs. Instead, it will be important to discover an extra element.

This type of creative value-added SME network is not expected to be built spontaneously. Therefore, the existence of some kind of coordinator or leader is essential. In Japan, by observing existing networks such as the local Chambers of Commerce and Industry, we can see the customary methods used to build networks that try to provide more value-added business. We can also observe the government-led initiatives driven by the Ministry of Economy, Trade and Industry or the Organization for Small & Medium Enterprises and Regional Innovation, JAPAN. Moreover, there are companies trying to build an SME network by carrying out capital tie-ups.

What method should be used to manage a network of SMEs from the perspective of a business process management approach? We have already explored various methods. In the first place, the moderate and loose networks argued in this paper do not assume a subsidiary position to any particular manufacturer's business like in a strong *Keiretsu* network. Rather, business processes run through the network and those which run through the sole enterprise are generally expected to coexist. In addition to their own business, it is the participation in a loose and moderate network that gives meaning to the network by providing value-added businesses that have a synergy effect. By strengthening ties within networks, the success of the business will also be considered. However, when maintaining specialized flexibility, the network tries to gain something extra by networking its benefits. The network does not seek expansion of scale by strengthening ties. Therefore, the method of management for participating companies wishing to network management practices should be selected in line with the intent of the network.

For example, in cases where the cost of building or participating in a network is high, deciding to participate in the network will be difficult, not only from the perspective of the SME's financial constraints, but also from the perspective of how to find the benefits. On the other hand, in cases where anyone can participate easily in the network, it is hard to guarantee the quality of business. Due to these problems, various management methods have been explored, and this could be topic for further research.

In my opinion, there are two points that must be considered and watched. One is the existence of a coordinator who can manage customer satisfaction, such as managing repeat orders or having the ability to respond to order changes. Another is the information that is shared by the participating companies. This information includes order price, cost, terms and conditions, ex-post customer satisfaction, and so forth. Through these two points, the return from such business is fairly allocated. Participating companies will also grasp the importance of taking part in the network and get a sense of understanding.

However, tightening the rules of the network is not aligned with the original direction or intention of an SMEs network. Without implicitly saying so, each participating company's ultimate goal must be to strengthen their own business. On top of that, to participate in a loose and moderate network, the company should create value-added business that cannot be achieved with its own business. This attitude brings more flexibility to the network and is the key to the success of networks, and is very different from the *keiretsu* model. The rules of the operating network should be built to maintain this flexibility.

From the vantage point of business processes, SMEs are needed to deliver products according to the demands of the final product manufacturers and must ensure and maintain customer satisfaction. In this situation, participating in a network of SMEs is expected to give added competitiveness to survive in a global competitive environment. And, this will also bring significant benefits to manufacturers. Hence, building a loose and moderate network of SMEs shall be regarded as the SMEs' new strategy that has supported the economy of Japan for a long time.

## References

Hironakka, F. (2007). *Technology Management of Small and Medium-sized Enterprises — Production that Brings Competitiveness.* (In Japanese) Chuokeizai-sha, Inc.

Lee, G.Y., M. Kosuga and Y. Nagasaka. (2006). *Strategic Process Management — Theory and Practice.* (In Japanese) Zeimkeiri-Kyokai.

Morishita, T. (2005). Strategic alliances strengthen the competitiveness of small and medium-sized enterprises — production. (In Japanese) *Shoko Journal,* 31(6), pp. 14–18.

Nishiguchi, T. (2003). *Small-firms Networks: Rent Analysis and International Comparison.* (In Japanese) Yuhikaku.

The Small and Medium Enterprise Agency (2008). *White Paper on Small and Medium-sized Enterprises in Japan 2008.* (In Japanese) Gyosei.

—— (2007). *White Paper on Small and Medium-sized Enterprises in Japan 2007.* (In Japanese) Gyosei.

# 4

# Global Process Management

Yoko Asakura

*Osaka International University, Japan*

## 1  Introduction

Enterprises expand their business overseas for multiple objectives. This enables them to extend their markets and obtain low-cost raw materials. Until now, these enterprises have given control to the bases in each country and combined results from the overall corporations are finally derived from the conclusion of each base. Consequently, each department or base has performed and tried to optimize operations to accomplish their aim.

Now corporations are under pressure to recognize and meet customer needs as rapidly as possible to acquire and maintain competitive advantage. Therefore, it is important to have the accuracy and expedition of data gathering for customer needs and promoting efficiency of the cycle to develop and provide products which respond to these needs.

However, as corporations separately manage each function-dependent department and base, it is thus not easy to create a process for providing customers with efficiency as well as high-quality products. As a result, the idea has emerged that they focus on the process from R&D to sales and distribution and try to make it efficient. This is known as process management and gives corporations more complex execution globally.

We will consider the method of global process management in this paper. First, we will bear out the basis of process management and the management inside and between enterprises. Next, we will go through how global process management in the enterprises is executed and the points that they must regard. We will also examine the methods of global process management among corporations.

## 2   The Basis of Process Management

### 2.1   *The concept of process management*

Process management has been defined by many researchers. For example, Hammer and Champy stated that "the process simply means series of activities that eventually create value for the customer and are needed by each other." (Hammer and Champy, 1993; Nonaka, 1993)

This shows that a process finally focuses on creating values for the customer and is considered as a whole series of mutually connected activities. Therefore, we will examine process management by defining the process as composed of dependent multiple activity groups and explicitly differentiating input from output (Monden and Lee, 2005) in this paper.

Furthermore, the management of these processes is referred to as process management. Process management is the management of processes by removing existing barriers among organizational units in enterprises or among enterprises, sharing information and management resources, linking operations, and considering the flow of operations as processes. This process management is divided into narrowly defined process management and broadly defined process management. Narrowly defined process management is across functions and departments inside the enterprise and broadly defined process management is process strategies across enterprises and borders (Monden and Lee, 2005).

The organizational units such as functional departments and divisions perform the operations to attain each objective in the enterprise. Therefore, a budget is assigned and a performance is evaluated by an organizational unit. In addition, each unit tries to optimize itself (see Figure 1). As a result, the unit reaches a partial optimization and most enterprises decrease profit as a whole.

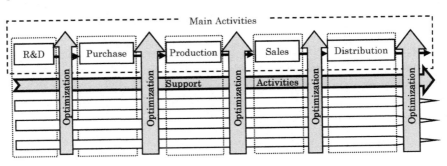

Fig. 1   Traditional Organizational Structure.

*Source*: Porter, M. E. (1985); Toki, H. *et al.* (1985), p. 37.

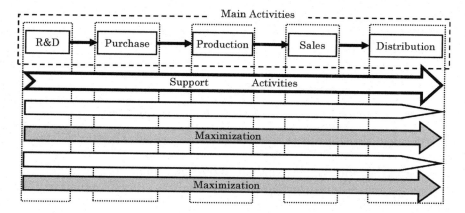

Fig. 2    Value Chain.

*Source*: Porter, M. E. (1985); Toki, H. *et al.* (1985), p. 37.

Now, a change in an enterprise environment is significant. Therefore, enterprises must accurately determine customer needs and rapidly meet them in order to acquire and secure competitive advantage. When each organizational unit pursues only its own optimization, it cannot handle such a situation. It is important to accomplish a total optimization of the process as a series of activities for maximizing customer value. Thus, we need to focus on the value chain (see Figure 2). This process management across function or department inside the enterprise is narrowly defined as process management.

The value chain is composed of a series of value-creating activities from purchasing material to selling products or services inside the enterprise. This is divided into main activities to take core corporate functions and support activities to support operations. Furthermore, the value chain receives added value and is eventually maximized in the series of this flow. To that end, we will analyze each activity, distinguish between value-added and non value-added activities, and eliminate non value-added activities in the process of the value chain. We will also allocate more management resources for value added activities.

In addition, the process strategy beyond enterprises or national boundaries (broad process management) is not only a process alliance among enterprises but also the selection, concentration, and affiliation of the process that uses shared services and outsourcing for the part of the process. That is, the process strategy involves decisions about the process to choose and focuses on both domestic and overseas locations based on their enterprise strategy due to environmental changes surrounding their enterprises (Monden and Lee, 2005).

In this paper, we will consider both narrowly-defined and broadly-defined process management.

## 2.2 *Process management inside the enterprise*

Process management across functions and departments inside the enterprise, known as narrowly-defined process management, not only focuses on activities in organizational units but also a value chain to quickly provide satisfactory products to customers. They need the system to support this value chain to achieve maximum effect.

The corporations need to execute the management with a balance between the "value chain" in the cross-divisional process and the "management chain" in which they apply the PDCA (Plan-Do-Check-Action) cycle to the organization performing the process to maximize the effect of this value chain (Monden and Lee, 2005). This system of process management is as shown below:

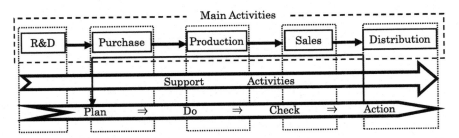

Fig. 3    Basic Concept of Management Chain.

*Source*: Porter, M. E. (1985); Toki, H. *et al.* (1985), p. 37.

Each activity in the value chain is managed by an organizational unit. In contrast, the management chain in the above is executed recurrently so that processes of main activities and support activities are maintained in the most appropriate context. Or, they repeat the PDCA cycle to cut costs and maximize profits in the process as a whole with the aim of maximizing customer value.

The more complex an enterprise environment becomes, keeping the process right becomes more difficult. Therefore, this PDCA cycle is frequently executed. This can direct processes non-associated to organizational structure to achieve the goal and balance activities in vertical administrative organizational units and horizontal processes.

Firstly, they set targets for each process to manage processes properly in this PDCA cycle. In addition, they make clear the scope of each activity and set performance indicators to accomplish the target.

As above, we need the system to evaluate the degree of contribution to the whole process as well as the performance of each organizational unit as usual. Members in each organizational unit can understand the role in the unit and process and perform operations in a balance by evincing objectives for optimization of processes as well as existing organizational units.

Balanced scorecard (BSC) is cited as the system to support this PDCA cycle. Given a managerial vision, mission, and corporate strategy that top management expresses, BSC is a tool that expresses key success factors clearly for meeting strategic objectives and links them with an operational control.

BSC provides the strategic objectives, performance measures, targeted number, and action items for each perspective (financial, customer, internal business process, and learning and growth perspectives). In addition, the items such as objectives and performance indicators in customer, internal business process, and learning and growth perspectives are correlated to attain the target in a conclusive financial perspective. Process management is the problem area associated with especially the internal business process perspective in four perspectives of BSC (Kosuga, 2003).

BSC can indicate what must be done in the process and as a result, how they can improve the efficiency of this process to maximize customer value and attain the ultimate financial target. Furthermore, it allows them to lead members in acquiring a skill to keep the process optimal from a learning and growth perspective.

## 2.3 *Process management between enterprises*

Enterprises have had to not only manage vertically divided organizations but also emphasize processes focused on value chains to meet the diversification of customer needs and aim for the maximization of customer value. For this process management, the point is management resources.

Now enterprises are unable to sustain competitive advantage if they do not respond rapidly to the change of the corporate environment. They consume more resources when this change gets greater. Not every enterprise has unlimited management resources, even if it is big.

Therefore, enterprises must maximally utilize limited resources and achieve an effect. To that end, they do not have to devote their energy to all activities and processes but instead select the activity or process of core competence and concentrate management resources on it. As above, the process strategy is deciding which process to select and concentrate on, on the basis of the enterprise strategy in response to changes in the enterprise environment both domestic and overseas (Lee, 2006).

In addition, they must handle activities that are not about core competence in another way: shared service and outsourcing.

Shared service refers to the putting together of operations in multiple organizational units and the providing of each unit with the operations. The productivity will increase by combining operations redundantly performed in many units. This is mainly applied to indirect operations and is used in many business groups.

Outsourcing is where one unit delegates all or part of the organizational functions or services to another unit. This is the consignment or outside order that commits all or part of the operations to another organization. Hence, this is where resources are externalized from the enterprise (Shimada and Harada, 1998).

As observed above, the enterprise utilizes external management resources and can effectively perform activities and processes other than core competence by consolidating or delegating operations. And it can focus the limited resources on core competence.

When enterprises expand into new markets, they may run into difficulties independently entering the market, depending on the market. They may also have to produce products of high value earlier than competitors, when they research and develop products with technical capabilities.

At times like these, they can effectively enter a market by forging a partnership with an already well-established corporation in the market. By cooperating with the enterprise, they will thus be able to develop a high-value product earlier than competitors.

As can be seen, an affiliation in which many independent organizations work together with aims such as sharing technology and risk is an alliance. They can reduce time and cost and improve customer value by forming an alliance.

The enterprise needs to manage the process as a whole, including other company's activities involved in the process, as well as their own activities, to use these methods effectively. Therefore, they need to perform PDCA cycle against operations in other firms separately from the radical cycle.

# 3 Global Process Management Inside the Enterprises

## 3.1 *Arrangement and cooperation in process*

Currently, most enterprises perform business in various countries, not only in their home country. Their purposes range from acquiring cheap raw materials and workforce to research and development for customer needs in each area. This varies greatly according to the type of products and services and strategy in the enterprise. For example, an apparel company producing and selling low-cost clothing procures cheap raw material, produced by a cheap workforce overseas and sells the finished products in the home country to provide cheap products to customers.

As above, the target in making forays overseas, the corporate strategy, and the form of business depend on which country and how the enterprise conducts its activities. Moreover, they need to consider the placement of activities after due consideration for the issues such as entry and exit barriers in each country. But the direction to research and develop, prepare raw materials, and produce and sell products would be common.

Thus, global companies deploy processes across borders for each target and strategy. First, in this section, we will study a multilateral process management inside the corporation.

The enterprises have to determine to what extent many activities in the process are dispersed in each country when they deploy processes. It is important to balance dispersal and centralization of the common activities in a whole enterprise because it is more efficient that the enterprise not disperse the activities but centralize them.

The corporations also decide where to deploy each activity. For example, in the case of R&D, if the product's customer needs depend on the country or area, they need to deploy the R&D base in several countries near the market to develop a product that reflects the needs.

However, the business does not have many excellent internal specialists with knowledge and technology for R&D. They cannot exchange the valuable knowledge and technology and have a chance of falling behind in important development, if they are dispersed in several bases. Therefore, they will need to organize a virtual R&D team, where specialists around the world can share the knowledge and technology with each other, even if R&D is executed in different countries.

This will allow them to adapt to customer needs in each market and simultaneously accrete global knowledge and technology. This is the same for other activities.

As observed above, it is vital to virtually coordinate each activity as well as disperse the activities to effectively perform the process, if they select an appropriate country or area for each activity and place it there. Or the horizontal flow of the value chain and the cooperation in each function beyond the framework of the organization such as divisions becomes important.

Thus, they have to have the information system to communicate across borders to efficiently execute processes placed globally. It is most important to communicate information rapidly for efficiency of the process.

Also, the corporations motivate members away from the home country and with different backgrounds such as language and culture to act in the knowledge of the whole process with each other in the process across borders. Sometimes they stop to make their own operations more effective and have to supplement other activities in the process. Thus, it is essential

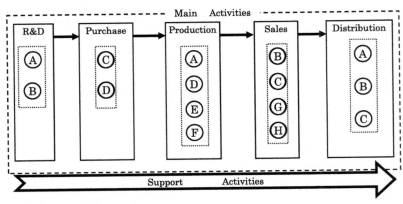

※ □ indicates a virtual cooperation.

※ ○ presents countries.

Fig. 4   Arrangement and Cooperation of Process in Global Environment.
*Source*: Porter, M. E. (1985); Toki, H. *et al.* (1985), p. 37.

to not only establish the information system but also set meetings to facilitate so members in the process can communicate with each other.

Additionally, now the enterprises need a person to coordinate or manage the whole process as well as managers in organizational units. This person will control the whole process to accomplish it without waste, aiming to maximize customer value. They also require persons to facilitate the coordination in each function.

## 3.2 *Process management and its problems*

Companies continuously manage the process arranged globally as well as the national process management by PDCA cycle. But in global process management, it is important to make members in a different country and of a different cultural background gain awareness of their roles in a process as well as in an organizational unit. This is more important in a foreign land than in the home country. Thus, it is imperative to first drive home the vision and strategy to employees with different language, culture and religion.

It is necessary for members in a different country to understand and thus be motivated by the target that must be accomplished by a process. To that end, it will be necessary to specifically point out the performance evaluation indicators and target and frame a reward system for a performance related to the process.

As above, it is vital to spread the vision and policy in the company to members in each country and clearly specify that each member has work to do in the process as well as in the organizational unit and the result. Therefore, BSC that can break down the distinct financial targets to each member would be a useful tool for global corporations, too.

Additionally, there are several problems characteristic of the global environment in managing global processes and aiming at total optimization. This affects process management as well as planning and performance evaluation in each organizational unit.

First, there is the fluctuation of exchange rates. It is important to maximize profits by making a whole process more effective and reducing cost as a customer value. A fluctuation of exchange rates has a great influence on measuring cost in a whole process. It would be necessary to manage in a whole process or enterprise and offset the exchange risk to tackle this problem.

And there is the matter of taxes, including tariffs. As enterprises place the process across the borders, they sometimes face big restrictions from tariffs for the import and export and a different tax system in each country when they seek the efficiency as a whole. This is a problem to notice at the time of setting activities.

As described, there are several barriers, including political risk such as condemnation of land, to come into and become prevalent in the market in each country. Therefore, it is not easy to manage the process over barriers and areas. They would have to repeat the PDCA cycle more frequently than in the home country and control the whole process to make these processes effective worldwide.

But a company alone cannot solve some issues related to global business. Hence, global process strategy including outside companies must be considered.

## 4  Global Process Management between Enterprises

### 4.1  *Process strategy across borders*

As mentioned in the preceding section, it is difficult for enterprises with restricted management resources to perform all activities and solve problems with global business on their own. One solution is to cooperate with other firms. That is, the companies have other firms to partially participate in each process.

First, they analyze each process and distinguish activities of their own core competence and other activities. They focus management resources on the activities of core competence and try to differentiate themselves to secure and maintain competitive advantage. They see if they make these activities effective in the process as a whole by the PDCA cycle as usual.

Next, the firms apply methods such as shared service, outsourcing, and alliance to activities without core competence in view of the types of the activities and the present circumstances. This allows the enterprises to perform the activities using outside resources and maintain the activities efficiently in the process as a whole. This is the process strategy.

Following that, they need to select the partner company from among many enterprises including foreign companies. In this selection, it is a given fact that the partner company performs the activities in an important country and area to make the process as a whole effective and offers a greater benefit than performing the operations in their own company.

Therefore, the companies first consider the type and current state of activities other than core competence and list the enterprises taking care of each activity in the area formed for the activity. They will select the partner company from among these companies by comparing the quality and cost of the operations that these companies perform with their own quality and cost. It is the following points that they must consider with this comparative discussion.

The first point is whether the enterprise establishes a relationship of trust to render the process as a whole more efficient. It is difficult to share internal information without trust, even if the firm's business outline is good. And they cannot cooperate with each other as part of the process without a confidential relationship. This is more difficult in the foreign companies with different cultural backgrounds.

Second, it is significant whether the other companies will establish an information system to share information closely or not. This is because the optimization of the process will grow worse than before by the addition of other firms without rapidly sharing necessary information.

These points for maintaining coordination with the foreign company vary with each enterprise. Thus, they must list the important points and select the partner company in consideration of them.

## 4.2 *The method in process management*

### 4.2.1 *Case of outsourcing*

The enterprises need to make the process, including operations the other company performs, effective when they use methods such as outsourcing or shared service. Consequently, how to perform the PDCA cycle is important.

In outsourcing, the corporation must implement a normal management chain including the activities of another company because they outsource part of the activities in the process. That is, they need to comprehensively coordinate their and the other company's activities and manage the process as if they are one enterprise. In what follows, we will consider process management among enterprises, for example outsourcing.

In outsourcing, the company should consistently evaluate the partner company to which they delegate the process in order to avoid inefficiency. First, it is necessary to establish the appropriate standard to evaluate the activities or companies to which to relegate the process. They detail several points that are important in a partner and present noteworthy items related to the points. And they evaluate each item in several stages.

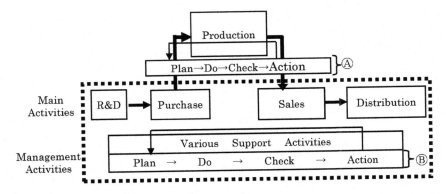

Fig. 5   Example of Management Chain — Outsourcing —

*Source*: Porter, M. E. (1985); Toki, H. *et al.* (1985), p. 37.

In this instance, they previously decide the base point for passing the evaluation and will have to look for a new partner if the company does not make the mark (Shimada and Harada, 1998).

This partner is evaluated in the PDCA cycle 'Ⓐ' of a management chain in activities to be delegated. It is necessary to execute this with a management cycle 'Ⓑ' in the usual process. Or they should balance both cycles by implementing the PDCA cycle in the process, including activities on commission, as well as the PDCA cycle in the activities (Figure 5). This is much the same for the shared service and alliance.

When the company which they entrust activities to is in a foreign country, factors such as currency or culture differ from the domestic company. Consequently, they should perform the PDCA cycle in view of points such as difference of corporate culture, the member's cultural background, the economic situation, or exchange fluctuations. And it is invariably necessary to monitor the partner more than in home country.

### 4.2.2   *The support of process optimization-BSC-*

As mentioned, enterprises must aim to optimize the process by working together with foreign companies as well as other national companies in process management across borders and enterprises. To that end, they have to repeat the PDCA cycle, including with other foreign companies.

It is to be noted that leading indicators as well as outcome indicators as a result are important in this case. Leading indicators show how to get good results. It is uncertain how another company can contribute to the total optimization of the process because they differ in culture even if they present the objective. Thus declaring the leading indicators will allow enterprises with different corporate cultures to work together.

And if the enterprise works together with the foreign companies, the members in the companies would differ in language, culture, and religion. Therefore, they must pay particular attention to these points because it is difficult to make processes effective for reasons such as communication problems among the members.

For these reasons, BSC would be optimal in process management. This is because BSC is the comprehensive management system for using the leading and outcome indicators. Moreover with BSC, they can spread the top management's vision and strategy to members in the other foreign company. BSC can additionally motivate members in each country by being a link between the degree of contribution to the process and the reward system because BSC can be in conjunction with the system.

If they use this BSC for a global management system, indicators in financial perspective must be measured in view of items such as exchange rates or capital cost varying according to country or area arranged process. In addition, they need to consider international transfer price, including problems such as taxes, too. It is necessary to use this transfer price in measuring by indicator in financial perspectives and evaluating the partner in the process.

And BSC will be able to indicate the kind of education that must be conducted for members (learning and growth perspective) to accomplish the objective in the process. Therefore, it demonstrates clearly the competence members in each base around the world and foreign other company should acquire.

Moreover, BSC can visually declare what objective they can accomplish (customer perspective) by achieving each target in the process. Additionally, the PDCA cycle in process management is integrated into the part of internal business process perspectives. They can comprehensively manage the process in a global circumstance by using multiple indicators in light of many factors for these three perspectives.

## 5  Conclusion

In this paper, we have considered process management in a global environment. Now enterprises target the market in multiple countries as well as in a single country. Therefore, they arrange the process of R&D, purchase, production, sales, and distribution abroad to capture the market. This management of the process is difficult in many aspects.

First, environmental factors carry great weight in arranging the basis of activities overseas. Such factors are variable and include exchange fluctuations, taxes, and political risks such as the condemnation of land. Moreover, factors such as language, culture, manners, and religion of members vary from country to country, and the background of members is different as well. Consequently, corporations must solve many problems to manage the process as well as traditional organizational units.

Additionally, other enterprises in the world may perform operations on behalf of them to make the process effective. These include outsourcing, coordinating shared service, and forming alliances.

In this case, the companies must shape the members of other companies to perform the activity in view of the whole process as well as the operation. This is especially difficult in other countries because they differ in language and cultural background. Consequently, the performance indicators and targets that make members aware of the process and system of rewards linked to it become important.

In this aspect, BSC can meet this requirement. They need to build BSC into the PDCA cycle in order to have members in other foreign companies understand the perspective of the process as well as organizational units and perform operations based on the perspective.

The enterprises can convert the vision and strategy of top management into terms that each member can understand by using BSC. Additionally, BSC is optimal for motivating members from other environments to achieve the same goal because this has not only indicators as outcome but also leading indicators that indicate what to do at present.

As explained, they must motivate various members to optimize not only the organization but also the process when the corporations globally expand the processes, and moreover when they do it including other corporations.

## References

Ansari, S., J. Bell, T. Klammer, and C. Lawrence (1997). *Management Accounting in the Age of Lean Production, A Modular Series-Management Accounting,* McGraw Hill.

Asada, T. (2005). *Strategic Management Accounting between Enterprises,* Dobunkan Shuppan Co. Ltd. (In Japanese)

Asakura, Y. (2006). Process Management in Global Environment (Chap. 5), *Strategic Process Management — The Theory and Practice.* Lee. G., M. Kosuga, and Y. Nagasaka. Zeimukeirikyokai, pp. 83–102. (In Japanese)

Culpan, R. (2002). *Global Business Alliances: Theory and Practice,* Quorum Books.

Daly, D.C. and T. Freeman (eds.) (1997). *The Road to Excellence — Becoming a Process-Based Company,* CAM-I.

Dowdle, P., J. Stevens, B. Mccarty and D. Daly (2003). Process-Based Management: The Road to Excellence. *Cost Management,* July/August, pp. 12–19.

Doz, Y.L. and G. Hamel (2001). *Alliance Advantage: The Art of Creating Value through Partnering,* Harvard Business School Press. Shida, K. and K. Yanagi (2001). *Alliance Strategy of Competitive Advantage: Partnership for Speed and Value-Creating,* DIAMOND, Inc. (In Japanese)

Fukuzumi, T. (2006). *Condition of Global Winners Enterprises in 2010,* Eiji Press Inc. (In Japanese)

Galbraith, J.R. (2001). *Designing Organizations: An Executive Guide to Strategy, Structure, and Process,* Jossey-Bass Inc Publishing. Umezu, H. (2002). *Management of Organization Design,* Productivity Press. (In Japanese)

Goldman, S.L., N. Nagel, and K. Preiss (1995). *Agile Competitors and Virtual Organizations: Strategies for Enriching the Customer,* Van Nostrand Reinhold. Konno, N. (1996). *Agile Competition,* Nikkei Inc. (In Japanese)

Gray, S.J., S.B. Salter, and L.H. Radebaugh (2001). *Global Accounting and Control: A Managerial Emphasis,* John Wiley & Sons Ltd.

Hammer, M. and J. Champy (1993). *Reengineering the Corporation: A Manifesto for Business Revolution,* Harpercollins. Nonaka, I. (1993). *Re-engineering Revolution: Operating Innovation that Radically Change Enterprises,* Nikkei Inc. (In Japanese)

Hiraoka, S. (1995). Management Accounting System for Process Management, *Sangyo Keiri,* 55(3), pp. 92–103. (In Japanese)

Kaplan, R.S. and D.P. Norton (1996). *The Balanced Scorecard: Translating Strategy into Action,* Harvard Business School Press. Yoshikawa, T. (1997). *The Balanced Scorecard: Corporate Changes by New Management Indicators.* Productivity Press. (In Japanese)

Kaplan, R.S. and D.P. Norton (2001). *The Strategy-Focused Organization: How Balanced Scorecard Companies Thrive in the New Business Environment,* Harvard Business School Press. Sakurai, M. (2001). *Kaplan and Norton's Strategic Balanced Scorecard,* Toyo Keizai, Inc. (In Japanese)

Komiya, K. (1988). Study about "Task Force Type Organization" — Availability of "the Emergent Project System" that Preserve Vertical Organization "The Unit of Gold Badge in Sharp Corporation" developed the electronic databook, *President,* 26(12), pp. 124–133. (In Japanese)

Kosuga, M. (2003). Process-Oriented Signification in Management Accounting (Chap. 10). *Organization Structure and Management Accounting.* Monden, Y. Zeimukeirikyoukai, pp. 242–264. (In Japanese)

Lee, G.Y. (2002). A Consideration about Framework of Business Process Management. *St. Andrew's University Economic and Business Review,* 44(3), pp. 23–42. (In Japanese)

Lee, G.Y. (2003). Business Process Redesign and Performance Management (Chap. 12). *Organization Structure and Management Accounting.* Monden, Y. Zeimukeirikyokai, pp. 207–229. (In Japanese)

Lee, G.Y. (2006). Design and Management Organization of Process Management System (Chap. 1), *Strategic Process Management — The Theory and Practice,* edited by Lee, G.Y., M. Kosuga and Y. Nagasaka. Zeimukeiri-kyokai, pp. 1–19. (In Japanese)

Mcnair, C.J. (2000). The CAM-I and Cost Management Integration Team, *Value Quest,* IMA.

Miyamoto, K. (2003). *Management Accounting in Global Enterprises,* CHUOKEIZAI-SHA. INC. (In Japanese)

Monden Y. and G.Y. Lee (2005). Framework and Management Accounting of Process Management, *Accounting,* 58(5), pp. 18–32. (In Japanese)

Ostrenga, M.R. (1990). Activities: The Focal Point of Total Cost Management, *Management Accounting,* February, pp. 66–84.

Porter, M.E. (1985). *Competitive Advantage: Creating and Sustaining Superior Performance,* Free Press. Toki, M., M. Nakatsuji, and T. Onodera (1985), *Competitive Advantage,* DIAMOND, Inc. (In Japanese)

Shimada, T. and T. Harada (1998). *The Practice Outsourcing,* JUSE Press. Ltd. (In Japanese)

Stonehouse, G., D. Campbell, J. Hamill, and T. Purdie (2004). *Global and Transnational Business: Strategy and Management.* 2nd ed., John Wiley & Sons Ltd.

Takeda, S. (1998). *Multinational Enterprises and Strategic Alliance,* Bunshindo Corporation. (In Japanese)

Tokuda, A. (2000). *Strategic Alliance in Global Enterprises,* MINERVA Publishing, Co. Ltd. (In Japanese)

# PART 2

# CASE STUDIES OF BPM IN JAPANESE AND KOREAN COMPANIES

# 5

# Business Process Innovations in Panasonic Corporation: A Case Study

Masanobu Kosuga
*Kwansei Gakuin University, Japan*

## 1 Introduction

Needless to say, most Japanese corporations are confronted with several opportunities and obstacles in their quest for creating corporate value. One way of benefiting from these opportunities and fending off those obstacles is to innovate, reform, and reengineer their business processes in order to adapt themselves to their changing business environments. *Business Process Management* (BPM) refers to a kind of strategic management systems based on visualizing several transaction flows as business processes.

The purposes of this paper are to sum up the main points of the research results of the case study on the BPM practices in *Panasonic Corporation* (formerly named *Matsushita Electric Industrial Co., Ltd.*) and to explore how and why Panasonic Corporation has been so actively pushing forward with *Business Process Innovations*. This paper is an integral part of a series on management systems and management accounting practices in Panasonic Corporation (for more details, see Miyamoto *et al.*, 2005; Miyamoto and Kosuga, 2006; Kosuga, 2007; and Miyamoto, 2008). The research was carried out during 2003–2006. In addition to Kadoma Factory (the principal factory located close to the Home Office of Panasonic Corporation) in *AVC Domain*, Air-Conditioner Division, Panasonic Design Company, and Vacuum Cleaner Business Unit in *Home Appliances Domain* were selected as main objects for case studies in this research.

Based on the survey of several publications on the Company, this study employed the semi-structured interview method. Interviewees were the senior financial director, chief operating officers, and managers of the planning department in its Head Office in Osaka, Japan (for the details of the Company, see Appendix). The following is mainly based on the descriptions in its *Annual Reports* published during the fiscal years 2000–2008, in order to exclude possible personal bias and/or misunderstandings.

## 2 "Deconstruction" and "Creations": *Value Creation 21 Plan*

### 2.1 *Core concepts of the plan*

In April 2001, Panasonic started to implement the mid-term plan, *Value Creation 21*. As part of this plan, Panasonic set a goal to increase net sales by approximately ¥1,400 billion. To maximize corporate value, this plan called for the reengineering of Panasonic's traditional business structures based on its successful experience in the 20th century. The core elements of the plan were as follows:

1. Structural reforms with an emphasis on profitability and efficiency improvements.
2. The creation of a new growth strategy.

Figure 1 shows the core concepts of *Value Creation 21 Plan*. The most important concept is the shifting of all focus to "creation" for a "lean and agile" Panasonic through *Deconstruction*.

| From: "Lean and Agile" | To: "Creation" |
|---|---|
| IT Innovation | Business Domain-Based Structure |
| Headquarter Reforms | Management Focusing on Cash Flows |
| Closure/Integration of Manufacturing Bases | Management Quality Innovation |
| Employment Structure Reforms | More Efficient Organization |
| R&D and Design Reform | Increased Brand Value |
| Reform of Sales/Distribution Structure | Global Strategy |
| Manufacturing Innovation | Black-Box Technologies |
| Corporate Culture Reform | V-Products |

Fig. 1   Core Concepts of *Value Creation 21 Plan*.

By implementing these strategies, Panasonic has been trying to enhance capital efficiency through the utilization of *Capital Cost Management* (CCM). CCM is Panasonic's own yardstick for internal divisional management control, and represents a type of residual income. CCM is calculated as follows:

$$\text{CCM} = (\text{Income Before Tax} - \text{Interest Earned} + \text{Interest Expense}) - \text{Cost of Assets Invested}$$

The balance of operating assets multiplied by Cost of Capital set at 8.4% is Cost of Assets Invested. As CCM is a kind of indicator for evaluating Returns On Invested Capital (ROIC), a positive CCM indicates that ROIC has met the minimum returns expected by capital markets.

## 2.2   *New Corporate Model: Super Manufacturing Company*

The aim of *Value Creation 21 Plan* was to transform Panasonic into a *Super Manufacturing Company*. A Super Manufacturing Company is a new corporate model. The attributes of this model are as follows:

1.  Outstanding strength in components and devices, backed by leading-edge technologies.
2.  Manufacturing products at speed with astute responsiveness to changing market needs.
3.  A firm commitment to providing truly customer-oriented services.

In summary, it is assumed that a Super Manufacturing Company stands for a lean and agile company, with the principal mission of providing customer-oriented services through the development and supply of systems, equipment and devices. In order for it to make the transition into a Super Manufacturing Company, it was imperative that Panasonic made itself truly customer-oriented and speedily responsive to changing market needs. As a starter, in 2001, Panasonic re-classified its business segments and established four new ones to adapt to changing markets needs and maximize growth. New segments and five areas of expected growth were determined. They were as follows: *AVC Networks* (*Digital Broadcasting Systems* area, *Mobile Communications* area, and *Data Storage Devices* area), *Home Appliances, Components and Devices (Semiconductors* area and *Display Devices* area), and *Industrial Equipment.* They were expected to facilitate strategic development of its business activities (for the details, see Appendix).

## 2.3    Manufacturing reforms: The first trial of business process innovation based on IT innovation

Traditionally, Panasonic operated its business processes under a system of autonomous divisional management. The Company established so many divisions by products, based on the basic principle: "One product, One division". In this type of internal management system, each division was responsible for development, manufacturing, and sales in each product area. Depending on the type of business and/or area for many years, so many inefficiencies had taken place in the Company as a whole in terms of resource allocation over several divisions that could more effectively have been shared among them.

In order to resolve this serious problem, Panasonic established certain independent *Manufacturing Centers*, based on IT Innovations, by separating the manufacturing functions from marketing and development functions of several *Product Divisions* and/or *Business Units* within Business Groups (such as, Home Appliances Company, AVC Networks, and other internal divisional companies). The Manufacturing Centers began to provide their services for various Product Divisions. Manufacturing Centers and Business Group and/or Business Units were interactively connected and integrated within electronic communication networks.

Furthermore, the Company conducted manufacturing reforms, such as the introduction of *Cell-style Production System* at various manufacturing locations, while reducing inventory, parts, and material costs. For example, Kadoma Factory, Osaka is the typical success case of introduction of this type of production system. As a result in the fiscal year 2003, Panasonic had seen significant benefits at all assembly operations in Japan, including a 90% increase in productivity per plant employee, a 40% reduction in lead times, and a two third reduction in capital investment.

Panasonic had also taken other initiatives to become a lean and agile Super Manufacturing Company, including the active introduction of *Supply Chain Management* (SCM) for management of products and factory shipments not on a monthly but on a weekly basis.

Panasonic had undertaken several reforms of its manufacturing processes. They aimed at achieving the following:

1. Manufacturing synchronized with rapidly changing market needs.
2. Lean production that can easily adapt to market changes.
3. Lean and flexible supply chain.
4. Common design platforms.

Panasonic has fully utilized IT in order to realize these aims. The Company did substantially reduce lead times in everything from R&D and design to parts and materials procurement, manufacturing and sales.

## 2.4  *Restructuring domestic consumer sales and distribution: The second trial of business process innovation*

The second trial was "Restructuring of Domestic Consumer Sales and Distribution" in 2001. The aims of these projects were to create a highly efficient structure so as to ensure agile response to customer needs, and to benefit from a cost reduction with an increased market share. In order to implement these reforms, Panasonic replaced the corporate consumer products sales divisions, sales functions within individual product divisions, and the advertising division with two new divisions: Corporate Marketing Division for "Panasonic Brand" and Corporate Marketing Division for "National Brand".

Furthermore, the Company consolidated several companies into a single company in several areas, such as logistics, credit sales, and leasing, respectively. By implementing these reforms, Panasonic Group companies as a whole positioned themselves closer to customers, tried to encourage taking responsibility for placing several orders with, and making purchases from, many manufacturing divisions and/or manufacturing centers, in adding to holding sales responsibilities, thereby ensuring speedy response to changing customer needs.

Other steps to realize a Super Manufacturing Company included the concentration of R&D resources through *Research, Development, and Design* (R&DD) *Reforms* in order to create new and competitive products, as well as management initiatives such as *IT Improvements*. In these Panasonic Group-wide R&DD Reforms, Panasonic Group established a common platform structure by creating *Core Technology Platforms* and *Strategic Product Platforms*. With this new structure, the Company was able to focus several resources on the development of strategic products that contribute to overall growth of the Group. The development of new typed washing machine by Panasonic Design Company in Home Appliances Domain is the typical success story in Panasonic Corporation.

## 3   Group-wide Business and Organizational Restructuring under *Value Creation 21 Plan*

### 3.1   *Main results of implementing the plan*

In January 2003, Panasonic reorganized their group structure to maximize the corporate value of the entire Panasonic Group. As a result of this reform, 14 new *Business Domains* were established. The Business Domain refers to a strategic large business unit.

This restructuring was aimed at providing the most effective solution services from a customer's point of view, eliminating counterproductive overlapping of businesses among Group companies; making optimum use of Group-wide R&D resources; and establish an integrated operational structure that covers everything from product development and manufacturing to sales, thereby ensuring a pertinent autonomous management structure. This structural reformation was designed to deconstruct its traditional management structures and create business and products that would lead to future growth. The Figure 2 shows the results how Panasonic restructured its business and organizations from the fiscal year 2002 to 2004, based on its Business Process Innovations.

### 3.2   *Roles of business domain companies and headquarters*

The key features of our Panasonic's organizational structure are empowerment and capital governance. Empowerment means delegation of authority and it is a prerequisite to achieving speedy operations with a customer-oriented focus.

Under this new structure, *Business Domain Companies* were established as customer-oriented and autonomous organizations. They have complete authority over and are fully responsible for all aspects of business

|  | "Deconstruction" | "Creation" |
|---|---|---|
| Fiscal Year 2002 | Domestic Consumer Sales and Distribution Restructuring Employment Restructuring Closure/Integration of Manufacturing Locations | Manufacturing Process Innovation More Efficient Organization |
| Fiscal Year 2003 | Transformation of Five Group Companies into Wholly Owned Subsidiaries | Management focusing on CCM and Cash Flows |
| Fiscal Year 2004 | Organizational Restructuring by Business Domain | Business Domain-Based Organizational Structure and New Management System |

Fig. 2   Main Results of Implementing *Value Creation 21 Plan.*

activities in their respective domain, of course including not only domestic but also overseas operations, from R&D and manufacturing, to sales. By delegating such responsibilities, Panasonic tried to promote autonomous management by each Business Domain Company, thus accelerating decision-making, and facilitating efficient allocation of management resources. Figure 3 shows the conceptual change from Internal Divisional Structure into Business Domain-Based Management Structure.

In 2004, Panasonic implemented further reforms to establish an optimum management and governance structure tailored to the Group's new business and organizational structure. Under this new structure, the Headquarters will empower each of the Business Domain Companies by delegating authority in order to expedite autonomous management. Purposes of this restructuring were to eliminate several business duplications, to integrate R&D, manufacturing and sales, and to concentrate R&D resources.

Based on this new structure, Panasonic revised the performance evaluation measures for Business Domain Companies to promote autonomous management and allow for effective delegation of authority. Their performance is evaluated based on two results-based measurements. They are CCM for evaluating capital efficiency and *Cash Flow* for evaluating a company's ability to generate cash. Both of these measures are applied to each Business Domain Company's performance on a global consolidated basis.

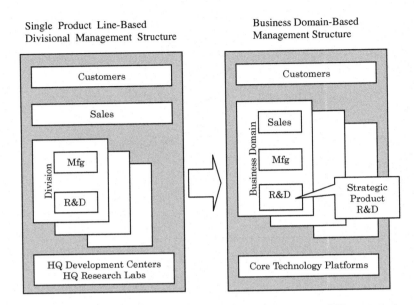

Fig. 3   Concept of Group-wide Business and Organizational Restructuring.

(Billions of Yen)

|  | 2000 | 2001 | 2002 | 2003 | 2004 |
|---|---|---|---|---|---|
| Net Sales | 7,299 | 7,682 | 6,877 | 7,401 | 7,480 |
| Net Income (Loss) | 100 | 42 | (431) | (19) | 42 |
| Total Assets | 7,955 | 8,156 | 7,627 | 7,835 | 7,438 |

Fig. 4   Financial Highlights: Fiscal Years 2000–2004.

### 3.3   *Crawling up from the bottom*

Figure 4 shows the financial highlights of the fiscal years ending March 31, from 2000 to 2004. It is clear that Panasonic was crawling up from the bottom by implementing *Value Creation 21 Plan* so actively. The positive influence of several reforms "Deconstruction and Creation" on its performance was distinguished.

After the *Value Creation 21 Plan* ended on 31 March 2004, Panasonic started the next mid-term plan called *Leap Ahead 21* in April 2004.

The aim of this plan is to achieve global excellence by 2010 to fulfill its mission of creating value for customers. The *Leap Ahead 21 Plan*, ending March 2007, represented the midpoint in this target for global excellence, and tried to establish a foundation for sustainable growth in the 21st century. Overseas Initiative within the *Leap Ahead 21 Plan* is a vital role of overseas operations as a "growth engine" in expanding business and enhancing overall earnings.

## 4    Toward Next Stage: Further Challenge of Future Growth and Creating Value: *Leap Ahead 21 Plan* from Fiscal 2005

### 4.1    *Initiatives of Leap Ahead 21 Plan*

Goals to be achieved (by the fiscal year 2007) under the next mid-term plan, *Leap Ahead 21*, were a planed operating profit to sales ratios of 5% or more and a positive CCM index, on a consolidated basis. The former was the objective to achieve a target of an operating profit to sales ratio, and the later was to raise the CCM results of all Business Domain Companies. These two objectives were set as the bare minimum for becoming a top global company.

The first initiative of *Leap Ahead 21 Plan* was "Accelerating Growth Business". Panasonic has been positioning V-Products as the vehicle of future growth. During the fiscal year 2005, Panasonic planned to introduce 71 new V-Products with a sales target of 1.5 million yen, compared with approximately 1.24 million yen in sales of the previous fiscal year's V-Products. New V-Products for the fiscal year 2005 were set as follows:

1.    Products utilize *Black-Box Technologies* that cannot be easily imitated by competitors.
2.    Products incorporate Universal Design Concepts to improve convenience for all customers.
3.    Products have minimal impact on the environment in terms of energy and resource conservation.

The second initiative of the plan was "Reinforcing Management Structures". With regard to R&D, Panasonic has been making an endeavor to strengthen their technological capabilities from a 10-year perspective, with the ultimate goal of consistently and continuously creating new value-added products and services. Through *Development*

*Process Innovation Management* (DPIM) at each Business Domain Company, based on the evaluation of ROI, Panasonic started to try further reducing product development lead times. This type of initiative tends to focus investment into strategic products, while promoting further efficiency improvements in terms of the ratio of R&D expenditures to sales.

## 4.2 *Growth Engine under Leap Ahead 21 Plan*

A "Growth Engine" planned under the *Leap Ahead 21 Plan* was consisted of several factors. They were as follows:

1. Superior V-Products, based on the universal design concepts, Black-Box Technologies, and environmental friendly features.
2. Continuous brand enhancement.
3. Result-driven R&D.
4. Strategic Investment and Business Alliance.
5. Reinforcing Management Structures to conduct further Manufacturing Process Innovations.
6. Accelerating IT Innovations.
7. Restructuring of overseas operations to build up strong overseas business.
8. One trillion Yen business in China.
9. Creating of a "lean and agile" marketing structure in overseas marketing function.
10. Corporate Cost Busters Project.
11. Reducing consolidated total assets.

Under this plan, Panasonic accelerated business and organizational reforms that began in the fiscal year 2004. The major initiatives, including the "selection and concentration of businesses" and closure and/or integration of locations, have been autonomously carried out by each Business Domain Company.

## 4.3 *Halving plant inventories: Cell-style production system*

Since May 2001, Panasonic has utilized a *Cell-style Production System*, mainly at domestic facilities, where the assembly of each product is performed by a single person or a small team. In the manufacturing process, Panasonic has achieved excellent results in terms of improved productivity and employees' job satisfaction. *Cell-style Production* results in distinguished improvements of cost-competitiveness by making several efforts to conduct continuous improvements, to shorten delivery times, and to minimize inventories.

In March 2005, Panasonic expanded such a system with a *Next Cell Production Project*. This project set targets for reducing inventories. Its target was set near-zero levels in order to enhance cost-competitiveness through continuous improvements, shorter lead times, and reduction of plant inventories. As the result, a structure was put in place to quantify production processes at each plant.

In the fiscal year 2007, Panasonic began to try utilizing IT in order to manage such initiatives as *JIT Production* method and *Vendor Managed Inventory*. The Company would like to promote *Production, Sales, and Inventory* (PSI) and SCM to reduce inventories of finished products, to shorten delivery times, and to reduce in-process inventories.

## 4.4 Management innovation through IT and corporate cost busters project

Panasonic has invested heavily in IT infrastructures over five years from 2002 to 2006. The Company has constructed *Corporate IT Architecture* (CITA) in order to serve as the standard and common infrastructure for the Panasonic Group. Based on this architecture, the Company tried to expedite its manufacturing process, strengthened its speedy response capabilities to rapidly changing business environment, and reduced several costs of information systems. In addition to cost and inventory reductions, CITA has played a significant role by shortening development and production lead times.

Panasonic had tried to construct a lean and agile management style. It reduced its consolidated total assets by 460 billion Yen from the beginning of this mid-term plan, by reducing factory inventories with the introduction of the Next Cell Production System, as well as accelerating IT Innovation.

In June 2003, the Company also launched *Corporate Cost Busters Project* aimed at lowering expenses on a Company-wide basis. By the fiscal year 2005, the project achieved its initial target. Panasonic began *Second Corporate Cost Busters Project* in the fiscal year 2006. It aims to

(Billions of Yen)

|                  | 2003  | 2004  | 2005  | 2006  | 2007  |
|------------------|-------|-------|-------|-------|-------|
| Net Sales        | 7,401 | 7,480 | 8,714 | 8,894 | 9,108 |
| Net Income(Loss) | (19)  | 42    | 58    | 154   | 217   |
| Total Assets     | 7,835 | 7,438 | 8,057 | 7,965 | 7,897 |

Fig. 5   Financial highlights: fiscal years 2003–2007

lower costs in every aspect of management on a company-wide basis. Panasonic began to try to reduce costs by approximately 220 billion Yen during the period.

Figure 5 shows the financial highlights of the fiscal years ended 31 March from 2003 to 2007. It is clear that Panasonic had been improving its performance. The positive influence of *Leap Ahead 21 Plan* during the fiscal years 2005–2007 was evident.

## 5   Core Concept of *GP3 Plan: Manufacturing-Oriented Company*

Panasonic Corporation announced the new three-year management plan, named *GP3 Plan*, on 10 January 2007. The plan's name is made up of three elements: Global Progress, Global Profit, and Global Panasonic. This plan sets up the management goals to be achieved by the end of the fiscal year 2010 including 10 billion Yen sales, ROE of 10%, and reduction of $CO_2$ emissions by more than 300,000 tons compared with the fiscal year 2007 at its manufacturing operations worldwide. The aims of this plan are to achieve steady growth with profitability and to reduce the environmental burden in all business activities during the fiscal years 2008–2010. This mid-term business plan guides and challenges the Company so that it becomes the global excellent company that Panasonic Group aims to be.

Another goal of the *GP3 Plan* is to use Group-wide innovation activities to transform Panasonic into a *Manufacturing-oriented Company*. With this aim, the Company began to promote wider collaboration across business fields and operating regions, and *Manufacturing-oriented*

*Innovation Activities* designed to reform the entire process of creating products.

The words "Manufacturing-oriented Company" means that the firm combines all business activities toward the launch of products, thereby contributing the creation of customer value. Manufacturing-oriented Innovation Activities are designed to bring about innovation across organizational and regional lines in all product-creating processes, including product design, quality management, procurement, logistics, oversea operating activities, and other operating areas of Panasonic Group. Panasonic is focusing on the rigorous pursuit of cost reductions. Adopting a company-wide process that seeks to rigorously lower costs from the earliest stage of product development, Panasonic has been able to generate profits in line with the initial plan.

This plan has three priority themes. They are as follows:

1. Double-digit growth in overseas sales: accelerating business development in emerging markets.
2. Four strategic businesses (Digital AV Networks, Appliance Solutions, Car Electronics, and Black Box Devices): maximizing group synergies to drive growth.
3. Continuous "Selection and Concentration": concentrating resources on competitive and profitable business areas.

## 6 Conclusion

In this paper, we summarized the results of the case research. The major findings are as follows:

1. Panasonic has reformed its organizations and management systems based on Business Process Innovations.
2. These reforms are supported by CITA, IT Improvements, and IT Innovations.
3. For innovation of R&D process, DPIM and R&DD Reforms are noteworthy.
4. For improvement and/or innovation of production process, Cell-style Production System, SCM, and key concepts such as Super Manufacturing Company and Manufacturing-oriented Company are significant factors.

## References

Kosuga, M. (2007). The relationship between strategies, organizational design, and management control systems at Matsushita, in *Japanese Management Accounting Today*, (eds.) Monden, Y. *et al.*, Singapore: World Scientific Publishing Co., Pte. Ltd., pp. 35–48.

Miyamoto, K. and M. Kosuga (2006). Management accounting in Japanese multinational corporations: lessons from Matsushita and Sanyo, in *Value-Based Management of the Rising Sun*, (eds.) Monden, Y. *et al.*, Singapore: World Scientific Publishing Co., Pte. Ltd., pp. 181–195.

Miyamoto, K., M. Kosuga, K. Sakate, Y. Asakura, A. Ohara, T. Toyoda and A. Kimura (2005). International management accounting practices of Japanese enterprises in the electronics industry: A case study of Sharp corporation, in *Management Accounting in Asia*, (eds.) Nishimura, A. and R. Willett, Singapore: Thomson Learning (a division of Thomson Asia Pte. Ltd.), pp. 189–204.

Miyamoto, K. (ed.). (2008). *International Management Accounting in Multinational Enterprises*, Singapore: World Scientific Publishing Co., Pte. Ltd.

## Appendix. Corporate Profile of Panasonic Corporation

a. Company Name: Panasonic Corporation (formerly, Matsushita Electric Industrial Co., Ltd.)
b. Head Office Location: Kadoma City, Osaka, Japan
c. President: Mr. Fumio Ohtsubo
d. Foundation: March 1918 (incorporated in December 1935)
e. Consolidated Net Sales (as of 31 March 2008): 9,068.9 billion of Yen
f. Number of Employees (as of 31 March 2008): 305,828
g. Number of Consolidated Companies (as of 31 March 2008): 556
h. Segment and Business Domains: see Figure 6

| Segment | % of Sales | Business Domains | Business Domain Companies |
|---|---|---|---|
| AVC Networks | 41% | AVC<br>Fixed-line Communications<br>Mobile Communications<br>Automotive Electronics<br>Systems Solutions | AVC Networks Companies<br>Panasonic Communications Co., Ltd.<br>Panasonic Mobile Communications Co., Ltd.<br>Automotive Systems Company<br>System Solutions Company<br>Panasonic Shikoku Electronics Co., Ltd. |
| Home Appliances | 13% | Home Appliances Household<br>Equipment<br>Lighting<br>Environmental Systems | Home Appliances, Company<br><br>Lighting Company<br>Panasonic Ecology Systems Co., Ltd. |
| Components and Devices | 13% | Semiconductors<br>Batteries<br>Electronics Components<br>Electric Motors | Semiconductor Company<br>Energy Company<br>Panasonic Electronics Devices Co., Ltd.<br>Motor Company |
| PEW and PanaHome | 18% | | Panasonic Electric Works Co., Ltd.<br>PanaHome Company |
| Others | 15% | | Panasonic Factory Solutions Co., Ltd.<br>Panasonic Welding Systems Co., Ltd.<br>Corporate International Trade Division |

Fig. 6   Business Segments and Business Domains in Fiscal Year 2008.

# 6

# BPM Practices in a Japanese Company: A Case Study of Canon Co. Ltd.

Yoko Asakura

*Osaka International University, Japan*

Asako Kimura

*Kansai University, Japan*

## 1 Introduction

The introduction of Business Process Management (BPM) into business operations can raise difficulties, one of which is resistance on the part of the employees at the workplace. Indeed, on-site resistance can determine if BPM implementation succeeds or fails. Of course, this is not just confined to BPM. In order to reap the benefits of any new management tool introduced into a business or factory, it is essential to have the co-operation, understanding, and acceptance of the workers at the site.

This paper discusses a successful introduction of BPM at Nagahama Canon. Through obtaining the understanding of its employees, the deployment of BPM was successful and the company's production efficiency was markedly improved. Nagahama Canon, a subsidiary of Canon Inc. (hereafter, Canon), is mainly a contract manufacturer of laser beam printers. For the successful BPM deployment of Nagahama Canon, it was fundamentally important to gain the understanding of the workers at the plant. This paper reviews how Nagahama Canon management won the workers' understanding and the innovative techniques used to gain their cooperation in deploying the new management system, critically important in any smooth and successful implementation of BPM.

Let us note at the beginning that this study relates to internal business processes at Nagahama Canon, and therefore pertains to process management (as apparent from the meaning of BPM), and not to process strategy. In this paper, our study will focus mainly on process management within BPM.

We will start with a brief overview of Nagahama Canon. Proceeding next with the case study, we will explore the factors enabling Nagahama

Canon management to gain the understanding and cooperation of the workers to successfully implement a new BPM system in the company. We will conclude with a few summary remarks.

To state our conclusion at the beginning, we find that the success of BPM implementation at Nagahama Canon can be largely attributed to the understanding and cooperation of the workers that were obtained by innovative visualization techniques. In other words, by showing the employees how the corporate environment would change and presenting them with easy-to-understand visual indicators, this enabled the workers to clearly understand the reasons for the change while boosting their morale and motivation.

## 2 Overview of Nagahama Canon

### 2.1 *Overview of Canon*

As we observed earlier, Nagahama Canon is a subsidiary of Canon. Naturally, the strategies and policies of the parent company have an enormous impact on Nagahama Canon, so we will begin with a brief overview of Canon.

In 2007, Canon commemorated its 70th anniversary, and reported record profits of ¥488.388 billion in the quarter ending December 2007. One can see in Figure 1 below that Canon's sales and current net profits have continued to rise for the past five years, and this remarkable growth is likely to continue in the years ahead. The Canon Group encompasses 219 subsidiaries and 14 companies that use equity method accounting.

Millions of Yen

|  | 2003 | 2004 | 2005 | 2006 | 2007 |
|---|---|---|---|---|---|
| Net Sales | 3,198,072 | 3,467,853 | 3,754,191 | 4,156,759 | 4,481,346 |
| Net Income | 275,730 | 343,344 | 384,096 | 455,325 | 488,332 |
| Cash and cash equivalents | 690,298 | 887,774 | 1,004,953 | 1,155,626 | 944,463 |
| Return on stockholders' equity (%) | 15.9 | 16.8 | 16.0 | 16.3 | 16.5 |
| Number of employees | 102,567 | 108,257 | 115,583 | 118,499 | 131,352 |

Fig. 1   Canon's Business Performance Over the Past Five Years.

*Source*: Canon 2007 Annual Securities Report, p. 2.
*Note*: Monetary figures calculated based on sales prices.

|  | Millions of Yen | Change(%) |
|---|---|---|
| Business machines | 2,438,011 | +3.7 |
| Cameras | 1,341,436 | +16.5 |
| Optical and other products | 309,640 | −14.5 |
| Total | 4,089,087 | +5.8 |

Fig. 2   Manufacturing Performance.

*Source*: Canon 2007 Annual Securities Report, p. 15.

|  | Millions of Yen | Change(%) |
|---|---|---|
| Business machines | 2,935,542 | +9.1 |
| Cameras | 1,152,663 | +10.6 |
| Optical and other products | 393,141 | −7.2 |
| Total | 4,481,346 | +7.8 |

Fig. 3   Sales Performance.

*Source*: Canon 2007 Annual Securities Report, p. 15.

Key business areas include office equipment (laser beam printers (LBPs) and inkjet printers), cameras, and optical equipment (semiconductor equipment, aligners, and so forth).

Canon's strong performance can be attributed to the management reforms and restructuring that took place after Fujio Mitarai became the President and CEO of Canon in 1995. Canon faced three serious challenges when Mitarai took over — product development and investment decisions with too much emphasis on sales and not enough concern with profits, weakening of the company's balance sheet, and an orientation toward only partial optimization of the different business areas in which the company operates (Niibara, 2006, p. 157).

Among the various reform measures adopted by Canon to address these issues, Nagahama Canon revamped its production system in an effort to improve the company's balance sheet (Niibara, 2006, p. 172). Specifically, Canon began experimenting with the cell production system as a replacement for the conventional assembly–line approach, and Nagahama Canon was the test bed for the new production system.

In the product sequence of development, manufacturing and sales, the Canon parent company focused on the development phase from the very outset. Although the parent company does directly run an optical equipment plant and assemble optical equipment in Japan, most Canon products are produced by one of the company's manufacturing affiliates. Similarly in the case of sales, almost all of Canon's sales within Japan are handled by the affiliate Canon Marketing Japan Inc., while international sales are handled by sales affiliates established in countries around the world. Within this overall scheme, Nagahama Canon is contracted to manufacture Canon products. Let us next take a closer look at Nagahama Canon.

## 2.2   *Overview of Nagahama Canon*

Nagahama Canon is a 100-percent Canon-owned subsidiary established in Japan in 1988. The company specializes in Laser Beam Printers (LBPs) and toner cartridges. Nagahama Canon is an Electronic Manufacturing Services (EMS) company, and has no development or sales functions. In January 2006, the company had 1,114 employees.

In 1998, Nagahama Canon was the first Canon subsidiary to adopt the cell production system. The system was adopted at the request of Canon operational headquarters at the behest of President Mitarai. The migration to a totally different production system was an enormous change. The process was a tortuous one with numerous problems, and the least of which being foot-dragging and resistance by the Nagahama Canon workers. But in the end, the changeover was a huge success, as we will detail in the next section. The number of units produced per worker increased to 1.13 times the old rate, and production value per square meter of floor space increased by 1.4 times the old assembly-line rate (Okukubo, 1999, p. 69). Based on the successful implementation of the cell production system at Nagahama Canon, the new system was extensively adopted by other Canon affiliates, and is now the mainstream production system at Canon plants in Japan and around the world.

Subsequently, Nagahama Canon was faced with another major challenge. Once the cell production system was introduced to Canon's production consignment factories overseas, Nagahama Canon lost its competitive advantage vis-à-vis Chinese factories that made the same kinds of office equipment products (Tanji, 2003, p. 23). As an electronic manufacturing services company, Nagahama Canon became increasingly alarmed as it watched company after company of the Canon Group shift their manufacturing overseas to China. This perilous situation triggered a second round of reforms at Nagahama Canon.

The key to this second wave of reforms was a fundamental change of attitude that spread through the entire workforce at Nagahama Canon. The first round of reforms with the deployment of the cell production system left many workers resentful, so the second round could not begin until this bleak atmosphere was dissipated. A key factor in successfully changing employee attitudes and boosting motivation and morale was visualization — that is, presenting the reforms and their beneficial effects to the workers in a clear visual way. In the next section, we will consider the role of visualization in the two rounds of reform at Nagahama Canon — the introduction of the cell production system and the recapturing of the company's competitive edge by reversing the lingering resentment of the workers.

## 3 Visualization at Nagahama Canon

### 3.1 *Introduction of cell production*

The cell production system eliminates conveyor belt processes, and "small teams of workers, or cells, assemble products from start to finish" (Iwamuro, 2002, p. 12). Because products are assembled from start to finish in cells, this form of production permits a diverse array of products to be manufactured at the same time and eliminates Work In Progress (WIP), amongst other advantages. The only catch is that since the entire production process is undertaken by a single employee or a small group of employees, cell production requires multi-skilled workers. Initially, as workers are not multi-skilled, productivity typically slumps when the cell production system is first introduced. Compared to the traditional conveyor belt system where quality depends on the equipment, the cell production system relies heavily on the all-rounded flexibility of the workers. A much greater burden is thus placed on the workers than on conveyor belt systems.

Before the cell production system could be implemented, a thoroughgoing spatial reorganization was carried out to eliminate all inefficient and superfluous space between work-places — a process called *majime* — even while the conventional conveyor belt system was still up and running. This concept of *majime* is multifaceted; it refers to thoroughgoing reduction of worker-to-worker, part-to-part, and worker-to-part spaces. The effects of this *majime* space reduction process are (1) wasted efforts of workers taking up parts or workpieces is dramatically improved; (2) the work to be done by a worker is confined because the work area is confined and stand-by waste becomes obvious, and; (3) line-side Work In Progress (WIP) is minimized (Okukubo, 1999, p. 55).

It was at this stage where the workers showed the greatest resistance. They were especially pained to now have to do their job while standing instead of sitting, having an increased work load, and having to work on holidays. What changed their minds was the total elimination of conveyor belts. In September 1998 when the new system was still being introduced at the sub-unit level, the first conveyor belt was removed (Makino, 2005, p. 7). That was tangible proof that the workers could see with their own eyes that the work environment was indeed changing and that the company was serious about adopting cell production.

Two fundamental requirements in implementing cell production are visual control and the elimination of waste (Okukubo, 1999, p. 60). Adopting visual control techniques makes it easy for workers to understand management objectives and targets, while eliminating waste improves the productivity of cell units.

Visual control is achieved by setting up various kinds of management status boards — Shipping Control boards, Production Control Boards, and so on — enabling shipping and production progresses to be easily monitored with visual signals. In contrast to conventional progress management, two points are deliberately emphasized in the visual notations: work progress measured in two-hour increments as well as the causes and remedies for disparities between planned production and actual performance. Proper places for parts, intermediate goods, and finished goods are clearly defined, and new intuitive terms refer to these places: the Store is where finished goods are kept and the Refrigerator is where parts needed for the assembly are kept. Management and control are achieved in a very easy-to-understand way by strictly defining the floor areas of the Store and the Refrigerator and exactly how the goods and parts are arranged. As a result of this close attention to detail, a lot of work in progress and inventory are dramatically reduced (Okukubo, 1999, p. 60).

Efforts to eliminate waste focus on two primary sources of waste: action/transport waste involving extraneous and unnecessary movements by workers, and bottleneck waste. Action/transport waste is eliminated by closely analyzing all movements and work performed by employees, then eliminating all extraneous actions that do not contribute to the value-added work of assembling the product. For example, wasted manual movement and movement to fetch parts are reduced as much as possible by positioning parts properly within easy reach. The elimination of bottlenecks had an enormous impact at Nagahama Canon, not the least of which was the effect that these efforts had on the mental attitude of the workers. When the flow of goods or parts in the company is held up or falls behind, this certainly does not contribute to the added value of the company's products. Obstructions and poor flow of products and parts give rise to inefficiencies and waste of management, storage, and movement (Okukubo, 1999, p. 61). In all the earlier discussions about Nagahama Canon as to whether inventories were too large or small, they never really grasped the concept of bottlenecks (Tanji, 2001, p. 61). They were certainly interested in the amount of inventory at the end of the month, but never gave any thought as to when inventories peaked during the day. The larger the inventory — even if for just short periods of time — the more space had to be provided. When Nagahama Canon management turned its attention to inventory bottlenecks, they were suddenly faced with questions of how long the bottlenecks lasted and when the bottlenecks were greatest (Tanji, 2001, p. 62). By dealing with these issues, they substantially reduced the peak backup volumes of products and parts at specific times. The elimination of bottleneck waste also led the company to change the indicators it used to measure progress toward goals. They considered whether target indicators for the reduction of bottleneck waste should be regarded as financial indicators or non-financial indicators. For valuing Work in Process (WIP), the company had always used the turnover period as a financial indicator (Tanji, 2001, p. 62).

Turnover period = value of inventory at the end of the month
÷ net output for the month
× actual work days during the month.

When focused on reducing this financial indicator reducing the value of inventory becomes an objective, which can be easily accomplished by converting "free delivery of parts to clients" to "charged delivery of parts to clients". In other words, the figures can be manipulated.

To fix this problem, the company adopted the number of bottleneck days as the target indicator when measuring progress toward reducing inventory peaks during the day. The number of bottleneck days is calculated by determining the inventory at the beginning of day before the (basic) inventory is used, the number of times deliveries are made during the day, and how long the deliveries take. Investigating these three factors — inventory before the beginning of work in the morning, number of deliveries during the day, and when the deliveries were made — revealed that the number of deliveries could be increased, the delivery times could be varied, and the basic inventory could be reduced. This way, the number of bottleneck days was reduced (Nagasaka, 2005, pp. 98–99).

Thus, the cell production system was adopted by Nagahama Canon. We noted earlier that, compared to the old conveyor belt system, productivity was significantly improved by switching to the cell production system. Thanks to cell production, the company was also able to reduce the number of employees involved in production at the plant by 207, and save 10,455 square meters of floor space. The success of the cell production reform at Nagahama Canon can be largely attributed to the visual manner in which the environment was changed which helped win the support of the workers, and the use of non-financial indicators that are easy to understand by the workers. We believe that using visualization and visual control techniques helped the workers understand what was going on through the transition, and was a major factor in Nagahama Canon's success in overcoming worker resistance and implementing the cell production system.

### 3.2 Ongoing production innovation after adoption of cell production

Even in 2001, four years after converting over to the cell production system, morale and motivation among the workers at Nagahama Canon remained low. The primary reason was that Canon had begun shifting much of its production offshore to Chinese plants. The cell production system had proved so successful at Nagahama Canon, that Canon introduced cell production in its China-based plants as well. Most of the Nagahama Canon employees felt that they had to somehow beat their adversaries in China. The employees were further demoralized because, as far as they could tell, the systemization of cell production had failed. They could not perceive any significant changes, so they focused all their efforts on short-term cost reduction. This set the stage for a second major round of reforms at Nagahama Canon.

In 2002, the President of Nagahama Canon declared the company's commitment to "craftsmanship (*monotsukuri*) solutions". The intent of this new paradigm was not so much to "beat China", but rather to declare Nagahama Canon's commitment to ongoing innovation in production.

To achieve the president's policy vision, the manager of the manufacturing division highlighted three policy objectives:

1. Vision: "Production is Sales".
2. Mission: "Contribute to EQCD solutions through production of LBPs".
3. Values: "Treat not just the end product, but the entire manufacturing process as the product".

It was critically important to achieve a fundamental change in the attitude of Nagahama Canon workers, not only to achieve the above policy objectives but also to overcome lingering resentment over the changeover to cell production. The manager of manufacturing at Nagahama Canon set out to change the workers' mindset and attitude with a new principle of environmental change that apparently laid stress on transforming the workplace landscape. The first challenge was to improve the workflow in the production process (Tanji, 2003, p. 27).

### 3.2.1 *Improvement steps to achieve optimum workflow*

After careful systemization of the steps required to streamline the workflow at Nagahama Canon, the "Improvement Steps to Achieve Optimum Workflow" plan was finalized in January 2002. Real improvement could only be achieved in stages (Tanji, 2003, p. 29). The ideas contained in the six-step plan were first tested on a partial model plant, and found to be effective at improving the workflow. The plan was then extended to the entire Production Division (Tanji, 2003, pp. 30–31; Kariya, 2003, pp. 45–46).

**Step 1: Reform Attitudes**
After setting the goal of improving workflow, the first step is to reform employees' attitudes to deductively consider the best means of achieving the goal. Piecemeal efforts rarely succeed in cases such as streamlining workflow that involves the support and co-operation of multiple departments, so it is essential to start with this step.

**Step 2: Organize**
Organize work areas by removing all non-essential objects and positioning all required tools, parts, and so forth within easy reach. Work is constrained by

how parts and tools are laid out, so it is a top priority to optimally position tools and parts to facilitate work.

### Step 3: Unify
Assemble all required tools and parts in one place. Observe the three principles of preparedness: the right parts in the right quantities in the right place. Parts only go in one of two places: incoming parts from clients go in the store, while parts needed for the assembly go to the Refrigerator.

### Step 4: Reconcile
Clearly define the flow of goods and parts — where they are coming from and where they are going to. Reconcile conflicts between the macro distribution and micro distribution of individual parts. Steps 2 to 4 are broadly classified as process improvement related steps.

### Step 5: Cycle
Cycling is the cyclical repetition of work. Rigorous cyclical processing detects inherent waste and inefficiency, since the minimum number of

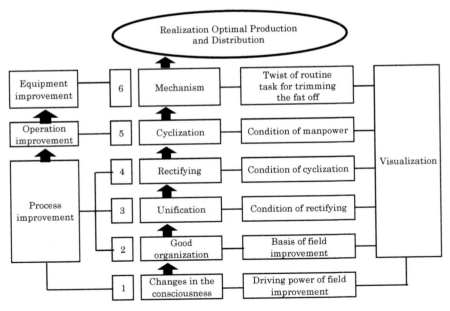

Fig. 4  Step Management to Achieve Optimum Workflow.

*Source*: Asakura *et al.* (2006). p. 15.

workers is a precondition for cycling while work that cannot be cycled generally includes waste.

**Step 6: Innovative techniques (*karakuri*)**
Tools and equipment are improvised to eliminate waste from repetitive tasks. This step of identifying real needs for improved tricks and innovative techniques is based on Step 5.

### 3.2.2  *Extension to entire Manufacturing Division*

Workflow enhancement measures were extended to the entire Manufacturing Division based on the "Improvement Steps to Achieve Optimum Workflow" plan. For example, after workers attitudes were reformed in Step 1, the layout of the Manufacturing Division was reorganized down to the smallest detail. The intent of the manager of manufacturing in transforming the workplace landscape was to change the workers' mindset.

All improvements are described using unique terminology that is immediately comprehensible to all the employees. Take, for example, the term Ichiro strategy. Since cleanup is indispensable to the reorganization in Step 2, this term is used to describe activities promoting cleanup. The term refers to the Seattle Mariners baseball player Ichiro Suzuki and his well-known tendency to properly put away and take care of his gear after every game. In the context of Nagahama Canon, the term Ichiro strategy goes far beyond just sweeping up the work area — every worker in the manufacturing division wipes down the equipment with a damp cloth every day. As a result of these improvement measures, the number of workers used to haul and transport material was slashed 30% (compared to 2001) and the inventories were reduced by 18% (compared to 2001) over a one-year period (Tanji, 2003, p. 31).

Subsequently, this same six-step process was used to improve the cell and Store sites. A Step Management Figure was developed to objectively assess the level of improvement at the different sites. This figure is also used as a diagnostic tool by the general manager.

### 3.2.3  *Adoption of Leaders Board*

When the cell production system was introduced, it was found that the Production Control Boards in the cells worked fine when motivation was

Check Sheet of Step Management Criteria (Direct Department)                                    Workplace name: Step 3 Judgement/Pass or Rejection

| Step | Items | Criteria | Checking contents | Diagnostics |
|---|---|---|---|---|
| Step 1 | Visualization (Changes in consciousness) | • Workplace is visualized. <br>• Core problems and goals for improvement have been identified. | • Does it fit the condition of the working place by using sheets including the standard working sheet? <br>• Do you receive an explanation about the improvement's core problems and goals, and is it proper? | |
| Step 2 | Good organization | • Ichiro evaluation "AA" is maintained. | • Is Ichiro evaluation "AA" condition and do you wash the dustcloth by hand? | △ |
| | | • There is a system to maintain Ichiro evaluation "AA". | • Is there a system to maintain Ichiro evaluation "AA" considered the best practice? | ○ |
| | | • The quality of the personal possessions locker's cleanliness is good. | • Is the locker of personal belongings cleaned up on an individual basis, and is deadwood carried on it? Or is deadwood left in the ownerless locker? | ○ |
| | | • The compartment line is fairly drawn, things such as equipment don't protrude into the aisle, and there are no fallen components. | • Is the compartment line properly lined out? Also, are things including wagons of products and empty cartons protruding and have components fallen in the aisle? | ○ |
| | | • The workers are well-groomed. | • Is grooming and appearance of workers in accordance with "The Basic of Grooming and Appearance in Accepted Basic Training"? | △ |

Fig. 5   Step Management Evaluation Sheet.

| Step | Items | Criteria | Checking contents | Diagnostics |
|---|---|---|---|---|
| Step 3 | Three-point management (Unification) | • The amounts of equipment, store fixtures, and industrial tools are adequate. <br> • The place of equipment, store fixtures, and industrial tools are adequate. <br> • The three points of REFRIGERATOR are managed. | • Are the amounts of equipment, store fixtures, and industrial tools in the cell adequate? <br> • Are the equipment, store fixtures, and industrial tools placed with workability, such as aspect and height, in mind? <br> • Is the displaying REFRIGERATOR accurately maintained or does it have too much volume of inventory? Also, are minimum and maximum display according to receiving? | ○ <br> △ <br> ○ |
| Step 4 | Routine improvement (Rectifying) | • Workers are operating using the same motion. <br> • There is no motion in which it is difficult for workers to pick up components. <br> • There is no wasted space in the cell. <br> • The operation of pick up wagon that used at post-process, is holding. | • Do you operate in a similar way when multiple people observe the three operations of the sample? <br> • Are you conscious of maintaining a fixed point and do you improve to enabling everyone to take components within the scope of reaching for above-knee and below shoulder? <br> • Do you have wasted space and distance? <br> • Do you observe the operation that subsequently processes the pick up wagon? | |
| Step 5 | Cyclization | • Time study of an hour per a day is measured and displayed on the leading board. | • Is the data of the time study chart old or is measurement accurate? <br> • Is non-cycle operation definite and do you take measures against it? | |

Fig. 5 (*Continued*)

| Step | Items | Criteria | Checking contents | Diagnostics |
|---|---|---|---|---|
| | | • Non-cycle operation is sorted out. | • Does the improvement action do for employee. | |
| | | • Improvement is performed by achieving actual efficiency of organization. | • Do you implement shopping lists on operational time and figure out available capacity per cell? | |
| | | • Shopping lists per delivery cell are created and available capacity per cell is figured out. | | |
| Step 6 | Mechanism | • There is an original attractive mechanism in each cell or each cell can utilize another cell's mechanism sufficiently. | • Do you have an original attractive mechanism in each cell? Can you utilize another cell's mechanism sufficiently? | |
| | | • The combnation of workers and operations is all right. | • Do you have points to be improved about a combination of workers and operations in the process flow? | |
| Step 7 | Independent improvement | • There are brakes for not to turn back from Step 1 to Step 5. | • Do you have items you can't perform from Step 1 to Step 5? | |
| | | • You perform items of the best practice adequate for your working place. | • How much do you implement the items of the best practice adequate for your working place? | |
| | | • You can understand the contents to make improvements later. | • How much do you record so that you can understand the contents to make improvements later? | |

Fig. 5  (*Continued*)

*Source:* Asakura *et al.* (2006). p. 15

high, but were inadequate when motivation was low. Although workers could already see the disparities between targets and actual perform-ance at a glance, Nagahama Canon management decided to enhance the Production Control Boards so workers understood the reasons for the disparities. This led the management to create a new kind of board called the Leaders Board (LB).

As illustrated in Figure 6, the Leaders Board highlights three Key Performance Indicators (KPIs): delivery, quality, and cost.

Deliveries are measured using a Daily Output Score Sheet. Much like the traditional score sheet used in sumo matches, if the planned produc-tion is reached within the specified time, a win is recorded on the score sheet. If the production goal is not met, a different notation is entered and the responsibility for the failure is assigned to self or other (e.g., a slow-down at another step). If a win is achieved with time to spare, the minutes finished early are entered.

Quality is measured by the indicator go-through rate, measuring the percentage that a product passes straight through the production process without delays due to quality problems.

Cost is measured by real organization efficiency. Real organization effi-ciency is the ratio of cycle time to total work time. The cycle time is calculated from time studies (to determine approximately how long it should take to produce one unit of product) carried out by the section head who is the cell manager. The time study results also serve as another evaluation indicator. While this indicator relates to cost, it is nevertheless a non-financial indicator.

The Leaders Board is used not only to represent worker targets, but also used by section heads to manage multiple cells. However, when the Leaders Board was first introduced, it was found that some cells did not update the board every day. Updating Leaders Boards every day is advan-tageous, because this enables problems to be detected early. This led to a new initiative to encourage daily updating of the Leaders Boards called the Meguru Leaders Board (MLB) initiative, in which the general man-ager, manager, and deputy manager make the rounds every morning to check the Leaders Boards (Makino, 2005, p. 21). This new Meguru Leaders Board essentially forces the cells to post their performance figures from the previous day to the Leaders Boards. In other words, senior supervisors assume responsibility for monitoring the Leaders Boards, and immediately checking with section chiefs and cell leaders in the event of problems. There was already a system of representing each cell unit with one of three

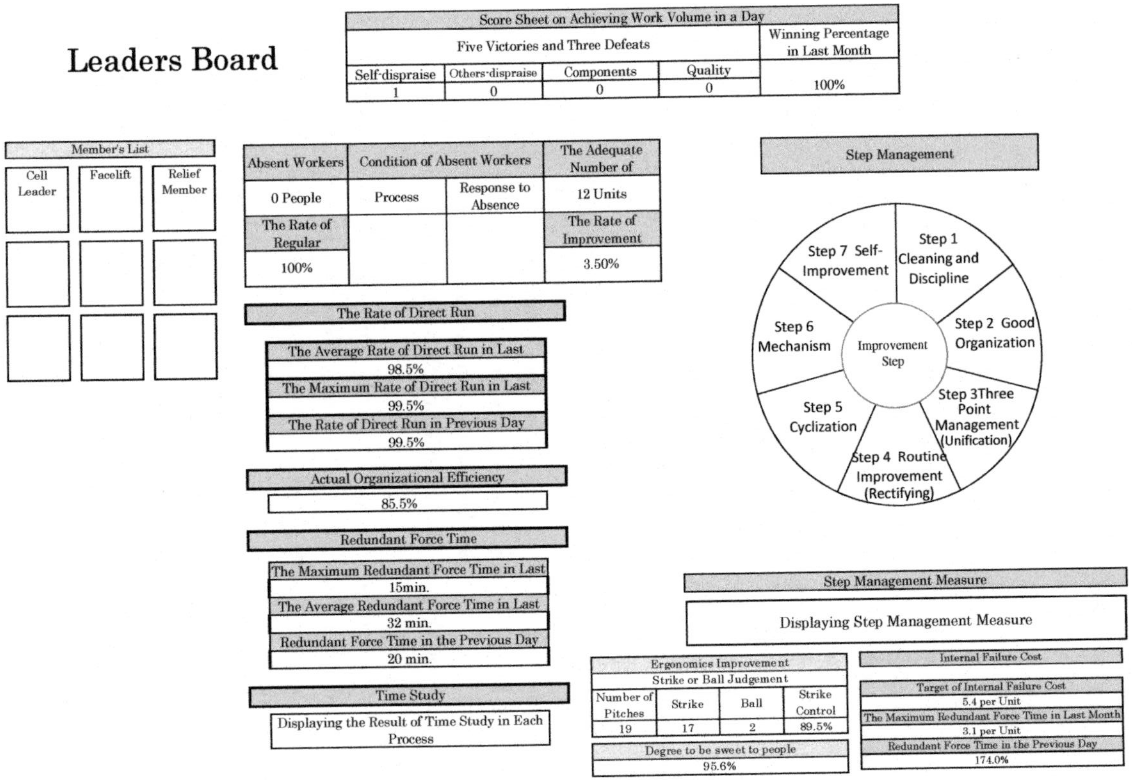


Fig. 6 Leaders Board Template.

*Source*: Asakura *et al.* (2006). p. 17.

colored flags — green, yellow, or red — based on the results posted on the Leaders Boards. Green means no absences and all passing indicators on the previous day, yellow indicates that a worker was absent and/or a failing indicator, and red means two or more absences and/or three or more failing indicators (Makino, 2005, p. 21). A yellow flag sends a deputy manager and staff member to the cell to investigate, and a red flag triggers a visit by the general manager and manager. The results are recorded in a four-column report (Tanji, 2003, p. 33).

### 3.2.4  *Best practices recognition*

When the cell production system was adopted, the workers made every effort to eliminate waste, coming up with all sorts of innovative tricks and techniques in the process of cross training and expanding their skills. Some of these ingenious new techniques involved individual worker skills while others could be standardized and shared within a cell or even by all the cells. To assess individual worker skills, a scorecard, called the Worker Skills Assessment Scorecard, was developed. To assess and encourage innovative techniques that can be standardized for use by other cells, a Best Practices Committee was established to recognize employees who come up with especially innovative ideas.

The Worker Skills Assessment Scorecard is illustrated in Figure 7. The workers are listed by name and graded on a five-point scale.

Skill Map/Table of Skill Confidence Coefficient

Skill Confidence Coefficient 9%

PA-○○

| Name / Process | Rank | 1st | 2nd | 3rd | 4th | 5th | 6th | Remark |
|---|---|---|---|---|---|---|---|---|
| Taro ○○ | S | AA | AA | AA | AA | AA | AA | |
| Hanako ○○ | AA | AA | A | A | A | A | A | |
| Ichiro △△ | A | A | A | C | | | | |
| Jiro △△ | AA | | A | AA | A | | | |
| Hanako △△ | B | | | | B | | | |
| Taro ○△ | C | | | | | C | | |
| Hanayo ○△ | A | | A | | A | AA | A | |

Rank of Evaluation
S:   All Processes "AA"
AA:  One can educate persons.
A:   One can work and resolveproblems by oneself.
B:   One can work by oneself.
C:   One can work with backup.

▨ Regular Process

Fig. 7   Worker Skills Assessment Scorecard.

*Source*: Asakura *et al.* (2006). p. 18.

Employees who develop an innovative new technique that can be and applied by all the cells are officially recognized with a Best Practices Certificate. Although this recognition is not linked to any system of compensation as of 2006, it is nevertheless expected to have three beneficial effects of (1) raising the work done by the whole workforces (the way of doing things) to the highest level, (2) properly recognizing developers and boosting motivation, and (3) engendering best practices in all the workers.

## 4    Conclusion: The Importance of Visualization

Nagahama Canon is adopting Business Process Management (BPM), a process management-oriented approach. Indeed, the introduction of the cell production system that so dramatically altered Nagahama Canon's production system followed by a second round of reforms well illustrate process management at the local plant level within the company. The hierarchical and functional lateral organizational changes at Nagahama Canon are consistent with the types of policies advocated by BPM. The Leaders Boards might also be considered a process mapping device for assessing improvements in processes. Considering the organic linkage between top level policies and onsite processes and the establishment of Key Performance Indicators (KPIs) and best practices, it is apparent that Nagahama Canon has pursued BPM to a fairly advanced level. It is just to say that the implementation of BPM at Nagahama Canon proceeded reasonably smoothly.

Yet in the majority of cases, the introduction of a new tool, such as BPM, does not go smoothly. The success in Nagahama Canon's case can be largely attributed to both the workers' understanding of the cell production system and their cooperation in implementing the system. Moreover, the active involvement of the employees in the deployment at Nagahama Canon can most certainly be attributed to visualization. The emphasis on showing the employees a tangible changing landscape that they can observe, the emphasis on intuitive and easy-to-understand naming conventions and indicators all served to promote clear understanding amongst them about the changeover to the cell production system.

During interviews, we asked about the effectiveness of the visualization approach to management using Production Control Boards and Leaders Boards. The respondents emphasized that three points were necessary for visualization to work: (1) the situation at the site must be known by the people at the site (they must have a true grasp of the actual situation), (2) the content of the boards must appear the same to everyone (shared concepts and perception), and (3) actions to effect improvements can be implemented.

In short, visualization is indispensable for the adoption of BPM to enable all of the participants to comprehend what is going on. Visualization certainly facilitates the introduction of BPM. In the future, we plan to investigate the importance of visualization in BPM with additional case studies and more detailed theoretical analysis.

## Acknowledgements

This discussion of Nagahama Canon is based on a series of interviews with Katsuyuki Tanji, Nagahama Canon's Managing Director of Logistics, in June 2006.

## References

Asakura, Y., Sakate, T., Nagasaka, Y. and A. Kimura (2006). The style of field report on BPM: A case study of Canon. *The Sandai hogaku.* 34, 11–20. (In Japanese)

Canon Co. Website. http://canon.jp/

Canon Co. (2005). *Annual Securities Report.*

Iwamuro, H. (2002). Cell Production, Nikkan Kogyo Shimbun Ltd. (In Japanese)

Kariya, D. (2003). Site Remendation at Nagahama Canon. *Logistics Business.* Sep., 42–47. (In Japanese)

Makino, N. (2005). How can we execute the self-organization of the factory, *St. Andrew's University Economic and Business Review*, 47(1), pp. 1–53. (In Japanese)

Nagasaka, Y. (2005). Logistics Management and Cost Management between Companies. Takayuki Asada (edit.) Chapter 5. *Strategic Management Accounting between Companies.* Doubunkan Shuppan Co. (In Japanese)

Tanji, K. (1999). The Adoption Effect of Stagnation Concept, *IE Review*, 40(10), pp. 61–63. (In Japanese)

Tanji, K. (2005). T-Project Creating Job Management Innovation, *IE Review*, 44(5), pp. 27–33. (In Japanese)

The Nikkei (newspaper). Mar. /29/2006.

Okukubo, Y. (1999). Production Innovation of Nagahama Canon: Good-bye conveyor-belt machinery. *Factory Administration*, 45(7), pp. 53–84. (In Japanese)

Shimizu, T. (2003). *The Challenge and Success of Innovative Company Canon*, Shuwa Sysitem Co. (In Japanese)

Tanaka, N. (2005). Canon intellectual property strategy for global competitiveness, *Business Research*, 970, pp. 21–28. (In Japanese)

Tanji, K. (2003). Developing field management by $t$-project. *IE Review*, 44(5), pp. 27–33. (In Japanese)

# 7

# BPM Practices in a Korean Company: A Case Study of LG Electronics Co. Ltd.

Gunyung Lee
*Niigata University, Japan*

## 1   Introduction

Process management across the organization became necessary and possible to carry out mainly because with the innovation of IT, information became available for sharing, and more importantly, customer power increased. Two articles triggered the remarkable process innovation that began in the business world — one by Davenport and Short, and the other by Hammer. These were both published in the same period during the 1990s.

At that time, the comparative advantage of U.S. companies was lost, so that change was required in order to restore their ability to compete against overseas companies' products, quality, and prices, especially when it came to those of Japanese companies. Davenport took up process innovation, and Hammer process reengineering, as a key for U.S. companies to regain their competitiveness in that situation.

However, process innovation was only the means which, after all, relied on best practices because it had neither a clear conceptual model nor a clear methodology. Thereafter, process management, in becoming a tool elaborated through IT innovation, moved from the world of art to the world of science to become today's Business Process Management (BPM).

Nowadays, there are two BPM methods: one is to review the workflow and construct a BPM model tied to the application software; the other is to restructure the business process according to the specifications of application software such as ERP when a company applies BPM. The latter approach gives priority to the application software, while the former gives priority to restructuring the business process. LG Electronics is constructing a BPM model supported by IT based on the former. I was interested in the BPM of LG Electronics because the company tried to develop its BPM system by reviewing the company's workflow, and constructing its BPM model.

Accordingly, I visited LG Electronics to investigate it for the first time in February 2003. I visited there again in March and August 2006, and was able to conduct interviews and obtain valuable information concerning its BPM system. LG Electronics carried out a pilot test, targeted at its export credit and marketing functions, in order to develop BPM system in 2004. Based on the results of the pilot test, the introduction of BPM was launched company-wide in the later half of 2004. It was after this BPM launch that it had became advanced when I visited in 2006. Fortunately, because BPM system had already been introduced a year or more earlier, the current state of the company's BPM attempt, and the direction in which it was headed to, could be investigated.

This paper presents a case study of the BPM system and the process of its introduction based on these two visits in 2006. In the following sections, the company will be described with an overview: first the mid-to-long-term strategy of LG Electronics, and then its recent financial performance. In addition, its BPM system will be discussed, and its process management organization will be examined in detail.

## 2  Company Overview

LG Electronics was established as Gold Star Co., Ltd. on 1 October, 1958 as the pioneer of the South Korean electronics industry. The products of Gold Star were only electronics, because the foundations of the electronics industry of South Korea in the 1960s were weak. LG Electronics, which changed its name from Gold Star in January 1995, got over South Korea's financial crisis in 1997. It then aimed toward a global business expansion that transcended national borders.

LG Electronics adopted a decentralized organization. It is now composed of four decentralized divisions: the Digital Appliance Division (with products such as refrigerators, microwave ovens, air conditioners, and washing machines), the Digital Display Division (with products such as TVs, monitors, videotapes, and DVD-R disks), the Digital Media Division (handling products such as telemetics, PCs, light storage, DVD players, and PDAs), and the Mobile Communication Division (with products such as mobile communications, transmission equipment, switch board machines, and mobile terminal units).

## 3 Mid-to-Long-Term Strategy of LG Electronics

On 5 January 2004, LG Electronics set up a mid-to-long-term vision, called "Global Top 3 by 2010", as shown in Figure 1. It aims at putting the company within the top three global companies in the electronics and info-dot-com industry by 2010 (www.lge.com). To accomplish its growth strategies, *Fast Innovation* and *Fast Growth*, LG Electronics has tried to strengthen the company by using highly talented people, in accordance with its enterprise philosophy of "Great Company, Great People".

Its *Fast Innovation strategy* is a strategy that ensures high competitiveness, of 30% or more, compared to its rivals. In other words, it is a strategy built to achieve the following goals — a target of 30% more market share than what the competitors can make, new product development, unveiling such products 30% faster, and developing technology to increase corporate value three years ahead of the competitors. And its *Fast Growth* strategy is a result of strategies designed to expand earnings quickly, while improving the growth rate in terms of monetary value rather than quantity.

On the other hand, *Product Leadership*, as one of the core capabilities, refers to the ability to develop creative, top-quality products using specialized new technology. *Market Leadership* refers to the ability to achieve the goal referred to as "the LG brand is No. 1", thanks to its formidable

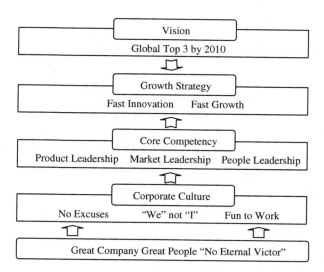

Fig. 1　Mid-to-long-term Strategy of LG Electronics.

*Source*: www.lge.com.

market presence worldwide. *People Leadership* refers to talented people, who perform extremely well by internalizing and executing innovations.

Furthermore, *No Excuses* refers to a corporate culture in which the employees must propose an alternative plan before saying "No", and in which *"We" not "I"* is a corporate culture axiom that encourages all employees to work together and form a strong team. *Fun Workplace*, another maxim of the corporate culture, is intended to create a workplace in which an individual's creativity and freedom are respected, and work is made fun.

## 4  Financial Performance of LG Electronics

The global sales of LG Electronics showed a growth rate of 116% in 2007, compared with 2003, as shown in Figure 2. Foreign sales expanded by 110%, while domestic sales expanded by 136%. Meanwhile, the operating income was reduced by half. The sales of the Mobile Communication Division accounted for about 40% of all sales, and the sales of mobile phone accounted for most of the sales in this division. In particular, the foreign sales of this division exceeded 35%. A detailed breakdown of sales by company division is shown in Figure 3.

## 5  BPM Framework of LG Electronics

### 5.1  *Target of BPM*

BPM at LG Electronics was introduced by the decision of top management to achieve the mid-to-long-term business plan called "Global Top 3 by 2010". During the introduction of BPM, following IT advancement, there

(Unit: Billion Won)

|                  | 2003     | 2004     | 2005     | 2006     | 2007     |
|------------------|----------|----------|----------|----------|----------|
| Global Sales     | 20,177   | 24,659   | 23,774   | 23,171   | 23,502   |
| Domestic Sales   | 4,794    | 5,086    | 5,509    | 5,947    | 6,520    |
|                  | (23.8%)  | (20.6%)  | (23.2%)  | (25.7%)  | (27.7%)  |
| Foreign Sales    | 15,383   | 19,573   | 18,265   | 17,223   | 16,982   |
|                  | (76.2%)  | (79.4%)  | (76.8%)  | (74.3%)  | (72.3%)  |
| Operating Income | 1,062    | 1,250    | 9,146    | 5,349    | 5,655    |

Fig. 2   Trends of Sales and Income.

*Source*: Annual Report 2007.

(Unit: Billion Won)

| Divisional Organization | | 2005 (%) | 2006 (%) | 2007 (%) |
|---|---|---|---|---|
| Digital Appliance Division | Domestic Sales | 9.7 | 9.9 | 11.3 |
| | Foreign Sales | 14.9 | 14.8 | 14.8 |
| Digital Display Division | Domestic Sales | 4.7 | 7.1 | 6.8 |
| | Foreign Sales | 16.9 | 18.1 | 15.0 |
| Digital Media Division | Domestic Sales | 2.8 | 3.1 | 3.1 |
| | Foreign Sales | 10.5 | 8.8 | 8.4 |
| Mobile Communication Division | Domestic Sales | 5.4 | 6.0 | 6.9 |
| | Foreign Sales | 34.4 | 32.6 | 33.9 |
| Others | | 0.7 | — | — |
| Global Sales | | 23,774 | 23,171 | 23,502 |

Fig. 3    Trends of Sales in Each Division.

*Source*: Annual Report 2007.

was a need for company-wide restructuring and management of business processes by IT. LG Electronics took the approach that the business process should first be restructured before introducing the application software, as previously discussed. That is, the direction of BPM construction, as shown in Figure 4, would be established. The introduction of BPM would be promoted, according to the following four instructions of top management:

1. Connect the manual and the indicator of each transaction unit screen;
2. Look for the expertise that relates to operations;
3. Secure interdepartmental, mutual agreement on operations; and
4. Make clear the terms of reference.

What is shown in Figure 4 is aimed not only at establishing a process-based operation system through the selection of accountable people for the processes, but it is also aimed at establishing advanced processes through standardization, efficiency, and the automation of each process.

## 5.2   *Range and system of process construction*

LG Electronics tried to clarify the processes of all its operations. The sections in charge of non-fixed works, such as management planning and so forth,

| Target | Urged Subjects | | Urged Direction |
|---|---|---|---|
| Establishing the advanced process of Global Top 3 level and capitalization of the process | Systematic classification of all company business processes | Standardization of process | 1. Standardizing the process and system among the headquarters, divisions, and foreign branches<br>2. Standardizing the nonstandard operations |
| | Making responsibility and authority clear by the process owner's selection | Efficiency of process | 1. Removal and unification of resembled or duplicated transactions<br>2. Exclusion of non-value added activity |
| | Continuous improvement of process base | Automation of process | 1. Digitalization and systematization of handwork operations<br>2. Paperless |

Fig. 4    Direction of BPM Construction.

expressed disapproval at first. However, most operations could be reconstructed based on the process because the relevant sections understood that the processes involved could be greatly clarified, even if they were involved in non-fixed works. The processes were systematized and reconstructed by using the process classification framework of IBM Consulting shown in Figure 5.

The company is deploying the processes following three steps: *Mega Process → Process Chain → Process,* as shown in Figure 5. The deployment up to "Process" is derived by using a function deployment method, "verb + object", although a Mega Process is a function division itself. In March 2006, thirteen Mega Processes, 250 Process Chains, and 1,400 Processes were defined and managed. The Mega Process was structured, unlike the classification at the primary stage of the BPM introduction shown in Figure 5. It was changed into the five Mega Processes of "Accounting", "Finance", "HR", "IT", and "General Management", in MGT, and changed into the three Mega Processes of "Service", "Marketing", and "Sales" in CRM. Finally, it was restructured again as 12 Mega Processes.

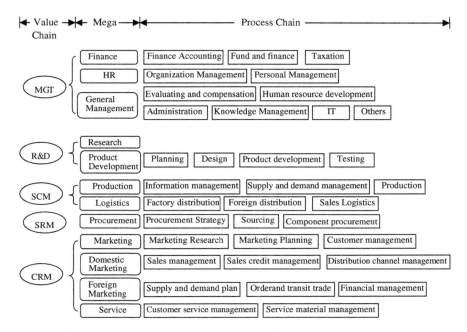

Fig. 5   Process Classification Framework.

## 5.3   *The main principle of BPM*

LG Electronics made construction rules for processes, as shown in Figures 6 and 7. The processes are managed by a Plan-Do-Check-Action (PDCA) cycle, accompanied by the establishment of a review system. To establish the PDCA cycle in the organization's management, and to improve the ease and efficacy of the PDCA management by IT support, the company is executing *Business Rule Management, Business Process Analysis,* and *Business Activity Monitoring* by IT, based on BPM. The process management system of LG Electronics is composed of a "process classification hierarchy" which becomes the base of the process hierarchy's "process analysis and standard template". This in turn becomes the support rules of process mapping and "the current state of the review and subjects" by the MPRB and CRB as the review organizations. Furthermore, the process is constructed by the composition principles shown in Figure 7.

| Corporate process base | Process classification framework | 1. Corporate business classification framework<br>2. Process title, code, owner, description<br>3. Level |
| --- | --- | --- |
| | Standard template of process analysis | 1. As-is process map (process definition)<br>2. Issue or analysis of improvement direction<br>3. To-be process map<br>4. KPI |
| | Current state of issue and review | 1. MPRB/CRB process, review items<br>2. Problems for improvement and current pursuing state of issues fixed through review |

Fig. 6   Structure of Corporate Process Base.

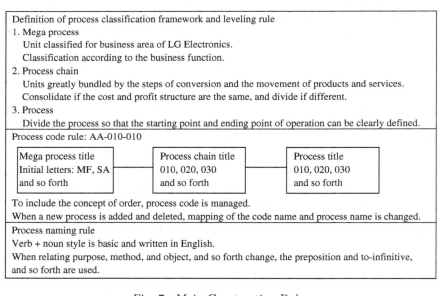

Fig. 7   Main Construction Rule.

## 5.4 *Process review system*

In general, a business structure specialist tries to design a flexible business system, and a system structure specialist tries to design flexible software. However, it has been noted that it is not easy for these two methods to produce a good outcome during dynamic corporate environmental change

(Howard and Fingar 2003, p. 3). That is, much computerized information is often not being used by the administrator because it becomes old as the environment changes. Davenport commented on just such a situation.

The administrator wants the timely information, even if this may be an estimated value. However, if the information is late though accurate, reactive behavior cannot be taken based on it (Davenport 1993, p. 74).

In the construction of BPM, the process management system should be integrated with an IT support system, and the process should be amended and improved at once, according to the changes in the business environment. If not, a job site will be separated from the IT support system so that the system will become a death asset. In LG Electronics, the

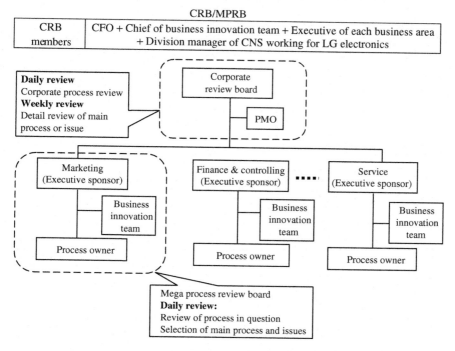

Fig. 8   Process Review Organization.

*Note*: CNS is a subsidiary for shared service of information management.

PMO = Process Management Office

process system and the process improvement activity are joined systematically, and managed in order to prevent such a thing. That is, to update the IT support system, a review organization, such as that shown in Figure 8, is created and managed.

There is the Corporate Review Board (CRB), which is the company-wide review organization, and the Mega Process Review Board (MPRB), which is the organization in the Mega Process area. The CRB not only handles to-be processes and the company-wide process review, it is also where the integration, adjustment, and decision-making of the company-wide process review are performed. The MPRB not only carries out process reviews in relevant areas and selects the main process issues submitted to the CRB, it is also where completion of the charged process review and the selection of areas for improvement are performed.

## 5.5 *Process-based organization*

The process-based organization is divided into the *Process Owner* who takes charge of the relevant process, the *Executive Sponsor* who organizes with senior managers to support process management, and the *IT supporting organization* that manages and supports the IT system, as shown in Figure 9.

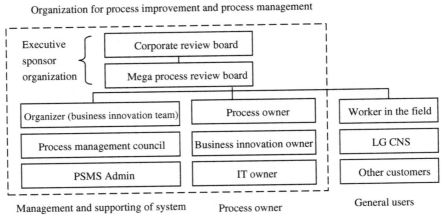

Fig. 9   Organization Structure of Process Base Management.

*Note*: PSMS Admin = Process Set Management System Administration

The following four items are the main roles of the Executive Sponsor organization:

1.  Empowerment to fix process revolution activity;
2.  Adjustment of the issue in the particular operation as the operation specialist;
3.  Being the interested party or the sustainer as the senior manager with responsibility for resource allocation to the concerned business division; and
4.  Review of outputs using the process map.

In addition, the following three roles are the main ones of the process owner organization:

1.  Promoting the organization of the process accomplishment and process revolution activities;
2.  Being in charge of process analysis, improvement, and execution; and
3.  Being the operator who takes charge of the relevant processes;

On the other hand, the management and supporting organization of the IT system takes charge of the following work:

1.  The management of the process-based organization and process-management program; and
2.  Monitoring the output and changes of the process organization.

Finally, workers in the field, as the executive members in charge of processes, are in control of it.

## 5.6   *The important roles of process owner organization*

The process owner organization has an important role concerning the adjustment of the process management and the change management systems. The process owners are primarily the section chief and the chief clerk. Each owner is in charge of two or more processes, because the number of processes is more than the number of owners. Each owner, in particular, has an important role as the accountable field person, related to the management of the changing process. Each owner's role, and work for which he or she is responsible within the company-wide management of process changes, are as follows:

### 5.6.1 Process owner's role

1. Doing process analysis activities according to various views, based on the understanding of the operation being accomplished;
2. Derives issues and improvement ideas as a result of work analysis, and establishing the program (World Best Process-oriented); and
3. Supports proposals for improvement of applications (operating systems) that users require.

### 5.6.2 Business innovation owner's role

1. Leading the improvement of company/organization members' performance; and
2. Capitalization of the business process.

### 5.6.3 IT owner's role

1. Leading the development and introduction of new solutions that satisfy the business needs of LG Electronics (maximization of productivity and customer satisfaction);
2. Management, maintenance, and repair of the IT system of LG Electronics; and
3. Leading the innovative IT activity of LG Electronics.

A detailed procedure of the work mentioned above for which people are responsible, and the specific accomplishment activities, are offered by the "BPR methodology" of LG Electronics. On the other hand, the process owners' outcomes are evaluated in the proportions of 80% and 20% for, respectively, business performance and process performance. Process performance is an outcome concerning process management, although business performance is an outcome of the business for which employee is responsible. In addition, the management indicators of the process outputs are divided into the management indicators and the outcome indicators, and the outcome indicators are related to the indicators of the Balanced Scorecard.

## 6   The Effect of BPM Introduction and Using the Information Concerning the Process

LG Electronics has used a process information and process map in constructing BPM for the support of its process improvement activities, its system improvement activities, the orientation of new employees, and so forth. In particular, by the job description cleared by constructing BPM, its process management regulations have been established, and decision-making is thereby made easy in the field.

On the other hand, changes before and after BPM adoption can be compared from the three viewpoints of business operation, business control, and performance as shown in Figure 10.

## 7   Conclusion

LG Electronics performed a pilot test for the introduction of BPM, and it started the construction of BPM company-wide in the later half of 2004. Such utilization of BPM was not accomplished without IT innovation. IT innovation, however, has to be used as an enabler of BPM construction. The promotion intentions of top management become an important variable, because BPM construction requires the investment of many resources, as was found to be true in the case of LG Electronics.

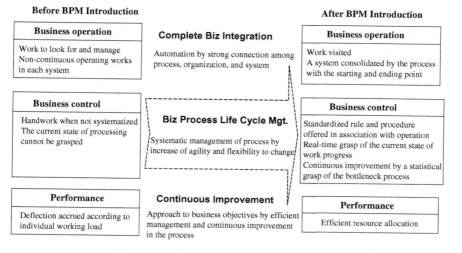

Fig. 10   The Performance of BPM Introduction.

On the other hand, BPM will become another means of securing a competitive advantage, given the corporate environmental change that has occurred recently. It seems that the problem of BPM in the future is how it should allocate and manage resources, and how it should evaluate the performance of that process.

## References

Davenport, T.H. (1993). *Process Innovation — Reengineering Work through Information Technology*, Harvard Business School Press.

Davenport, T.H. and J.E. Short. (1990). The New Industrial Engineering Information Technology and Business Process Redesign, *Sloan Management Review*, Summer, 31(4), pp. 11–27.

Hammer, M. (1990). Reengineering Work: Don't Automate, Obliterate, *Harvard Business Review*, July–August, pp. 104–112.

Howard, S. and P. Fingar. (2003). *Business Process Management: The Third Wave*, Meghan-Kiffer Press.

# 8
# Business Process Management: A Case of Korea Telecommunication Co. (KT)

Byungkyu Sohn
*Sookmyung Women's University, South Korea*

## 1 Introduction

Continuously changing business environments can be either an opportunity or challenge for companies. In recent years, two of the greatest changes might be the advancement of digital technology and the globalization of market due to the market opening of many nations. The advancement of digital technology has been led by the invention of the computer. The capability of the computer has expanded rapidly as Gordon Moore, a scholar in Fairchild in 1965, predicted that the capacity of microchip would be doubled every 18 months. The computer has greatly influenced firms not only on their products and manufacturing technologies but also on their business environment. With regard to globalization of markets, money and goods of firms are moving freely from one nation to another. The result is that almost all local markets that have been integrated into one large market that encompasses the whole world. These changes provided firms the opportunity of expanding the markets of their products; however, they also brought cut-throat competitions to them. Besieged with these changes, firms have made efforts to respond to them effectively, which have spawned many management innovation initiatives.

The innovation and improvement on process have been concerns to firms for long; however, it is in recent years that it receives more interest than ever. Mass production system that utilizes conveyor belt invented by Ford in the early 20th century is a representative case of process innovation, which dramatically improved productivity of automobile production. Since then, process innovation has not come to the center of management innovation. It might be Hammer and Champy who brought the process back to the focus of management innovation when they promoted Business Process Reengineering (BPR) in 1993. The key concept of BPR is to reduce waste to the minimum by reengineering work processes from the scratch. Its major contribution was that it could attract the firms' attention to the importance of process. However, it was criticized that it could not provide a concrete methodology. After that, a strong demand for slim organization and process strategy using IT technology was on the rise in order to overcome depressed economy. As a result, the methods such as Activity Based Management (ABM), Supply Chain Management (SCM), and Balanced Score Card (BSC) were introduced, followed by Business Process Management (BPM) in recent years. BPM is defined as the management of overall activities of planning, improving, and re-designing processes to fortify the competitiveness of company. It differs from BPR in the sense that it maintains and improves existing processes rather than creating a new process. Elliot, Pautz and Chauncey defined BPM as a framework that gives responsiveness and authority to the owner of process and manages one or several processes to meet the needs of customers.

This paper presents a case study of how KT, a Korean firm, applies BPM. KT belongs to the telecommunication industry which is leading business environment changes of today. Furthermore, KT is in the driving seat leading the changes in the industry, and at the same time it needs to adjust to the changing environment. Therefore, it is very interesting and meaningful to analyze the company. The ultimate purpose of BPM is to satisfy customers by renovating the processes in order to eliminate wastes residing in inefficient processes. Moreover, BPM attempts to evaluate, maintain, and grow the renovated processes. KT, which was privatized from a public corporation, had to focus on customer satisfaction to survive in competition. Therefore, KT needed competency to provide the maximum value to the customers through process innovation.

In this paper, the history of KT is reviewed first, followed by the explanation of background and the phases of introducing BPM. Then, the overall system of KT's BPM and the ways in which the two chosen illustrative processes are implemented will be studied.

## 2   History of KT

### 2.1   *Development and growth of KT*

The origin of KT was the communication business division of Department of Postal Services, which was a government ministry. It was separated from the department to become Korea Electric and Telecommunication Corp. in 1981 as a public company with the mission of promoting public welfare. Its initial efforts were centered on the establishment of telephone service infrastructure. The number of telephone lines which was only 4.5 million in 1982, boosted to 20 million in 1993 by virtue of a successful localization of telephone switch equipments in 1984. As the internet technology spread widely in the 1990s, KT invested heavily on the expansion of internet infrastructure. The result was that KT could have its internet network and satellite communication system of high technology in 1994. In 1997, KT started to expand its business scope from wired telephone business toward wireless and internet business. For the internet service, KT focused their capacities on building up the foundation of internet network through introduction of ADSL and super-speed national network. KT bought up HansolM.com in 2000 and then founded KTF, a subsidiary company for wireless communication service in 2001.

In the 1980s, many nations began to deregulate and privatize public enterprises for the purpose of promoting free market economy. The privatization of British Telecom (BT) in 1984 catalysed similar actions in the telecommunication industry from all over the world. Korea drove the privatization movement by deciding to sell the government-owned stocks of KT. However, its implementation was postponed due to the depressed stock market at the time. KT stocks began to be traded in the stock market in 1998, and its privatization process progressed in a speedy manner. Complete privatization of KT was achieved in 2002 when the entire ownership of the government was sold out. While this process was under way, KT changed its name to 'KT' and proclaimed new CI in 2001. It began to hold the top position in the domestic super-speed internet market share by focusing their competences on the internet business. Figure 1 shows KT's market share in its major business areas. Figure 1 indentified that KT is in the absolute predominant position in the traditional business

| Section | 2000 | 2001 | 2002 | 2003 | 2004 | 2005 | 2006 | 2007 |
|---|---|---|---|---|---|---|---|---|
| Local-call | 98.3 | 97.0 | 96.0 | 95.6 | 93.8 | 93.2 | 92.1 | 90.4 |
| Long-distance call | 83.4 | 80.9 | 80.4 | 84.3 | 84.4 | 85.4 | 85.6 | 85.4 |
| International call | 49.5 | 47.0 | 46.3 | 39.7 | 38.9 | 41.3 | —* | —* |
| Super-speed internet | 43.9 | 49.4 | 47.3 | 50.0 | 51.0 | 51.2 | 45.2 | 44.3 |

Fig. 1    Domestic Market Share of KT in Major Business (in %).
*Note*: * Implies unavailability of data.
*Source*: KT's CSR Reports (2006, 2007, 2008).

| Section | 2002 | 2003 | 2004 | 2005 | 2006 | 2007 |
|---|---|---|---|---|---|---|
| Sales | 117,088 | 115,745 | 118,508 | 118,773 | 118,560 | 119,364 |
| Net profit | 19,638 | 8,301 | 12,555 | 9,973 | 12,334 | 9,576 |

Fig. 2  Annual Sales of KT (in hundred million won).

*Source*: KT's Annual Reports (2006, 2007, 2008).

areas of local and long-distance calls. In addition, in the super-speed internet business where KT entered late, KT was able to increase its market share remarkably in just one year since the start-up. Such a rapid growth is attributed to its already owned local telephone network, which KT utilized to provide internet service in ADSL manner.

The sales of KT are summarized in Figure 2. Since 2000, sales in the wired telephone business have decreased gradually while that of the internet and wireless telephone businesses improved slowly, with overall sales remaining stable. Although the net profit has been fluctuating temporarily, its overall trend is pretty flat. This denotes that the telecommunication industry which KT belongs to is approaching the stage of maturity.

## 2.2  Business strategy and innovation

### 2.2.1  Vision and corporate strategy of KT

The main feature of telecommunication industry which KT belongs to is its rapidly changing technology, which makes it difficult to predict its future orientation. This feature can be considered as new market opportunity to firms in a certain aspect; however, it is a risk of exposure to future uncertainty at the same time. To cope with both sides of the feature effectively, KT developed the policy called "Future Strategy 2010". KT predicted the society of 2010 as an "ubiquitous" society where information can move freely beyond the limits of time and space. Ubiquitous society can be realized in four spaces of individual human being, home, office, and mobility. In these spaces, people can communicate and share information anywhere and anytime. KT prospects that an "Ubiquitous Life" will support each individual with all the necessary information to utilize his/her capabilities fully. Further, in the family space, all the information and electronic machines are connected with home networking to enhance the benefit for various needs of life, which is called "Ubiquitous Home". An "Ubiquitous Office" provides all the information to promote the efficiency and productivity of work at office.

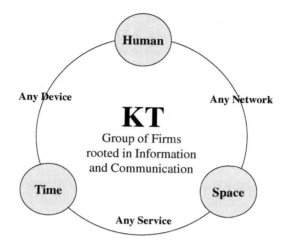

Fig. 3    Roles of KT in "Future Strategy 2010".

"Ubiquitous Mobility" will be realized so as to control and utilize every kind of information and services anywhere at any time.

As Figure 3 demonstrates, the vision of KT is to play the central role of connecting anybody at any time and any place in the future ubiquitous society. In order to achieve the vision, KT embodied their businesses in three major areas — key businesses, newly growing businesses, additional entry businesses. KT tries to reinforce the key businesses which involve telephone business, the super-speed internet business, integrated services with wired and wireless networks, and bundle services with dynamic mix of major KT business. For newly growing businesses, KT identified next generation mobile communication like Wibro, Home Networking which provides total service to customers at home. It also includes the business that distributes digital contents by integrating communication and broadcasting, IT consulting service for corporate customers, distribution and circulation of digital contents. Additional entry businesses are those which can bring synergy effects with current major businesses in KT by utilizing human and material resources. They include the ones such as RFID, u-Sensing, or u-Computing, through which KT tries to expand its business areas.

### 2.2.2   *Business innovation in KT*

A common business philosophy in recent years is "Management for Customer Satisfaction". KT also made all the efforts to achieve customer satisfaction since it changed its name to "KT" in 2001. Management for customer satisfaction require the firm to think from the customers' perspective in order to satisfy customers' needs and to provide new values to customers. KT's management for customer satisfaction evolved from "One Heart Movement" for service innovation from 1989, and then moved to "Customer Satisfaction Movement" from 1994 to 2002. While past customer satisfaction initiatives focused only on service kindness, the next initiative since 2003 accelerated true customer satisfaction with the leadership from Quality Management Team directly responsible to CEO. At this phase, they focused on three things as follows:

1.  KT recognized the importance of internal customers as well as external customers. It then conducted Customer Service (CS) training program for employees throughout the years, and also provided a consulting needed to perform their tasks effectively. Moreover, KT established a reward system linked to performance, and diversified the channels of internal communication;

2.  KT developed a measurement system for Customer Satisfaction which evaluates the conformity of CS management. The firm also organized a Quality Management Team which directs company-wide activities of CS management by planning, evaluating, and improving those activities; and

3.  For continuous improvement, KT focused on "VOC as a resource of management" which reflects voice of customers without filtering. Then it tried to create customers' value through process improvement in response to customers' complaints.

KT revised its business strategy in 2006, clarifying its two major goals as growth and innovation. For the goal of growth, the firm emphasized the strengthening of the base for its competency. KT reviewed its product strategy, distribution network strategy, and its system for analyzing customer needs. For the goal of innovation, KT pursued management infrastructure reengineering in four dimensions which are organization, human, process, and corporation culture. The specific methods used for the innovation are Management Quality modified from U.S. Malcomb Baldridge National Quality Award model, Six Sigma, and Process Innovation.

Six Sigma has been adopted by KT since 2000. The spirits of the Six Sigma initiative are: 1) customer oriented management which responds fully to customers' requirement; 2) elimination of wastes through creative thinking; and 3) development of learning organization that grows continually.

KT adopted the Six Sigma initiative to effectively respond to the changes in telecommunication industry, especially the changes in technology and customers' requirements. The Quality Management Team, that is responsible for the Six Sigma initiative, established the ground for continuous improvement with Six Sigma school, human resource system for Six Sigma projects, new reward and supporting system. The Six Sigma movement in KT is a companywide campaign. The first stage called "The 1st Wave" focused on creating innovative minds throughout the company. The result of this movement was notable. The financial performance from the 1st Wave that was held from June to December in 2003 was assessed at about 41 billion Korean won. This achievement was made through sales increase, cost reduction, waste reduction, and savings in investment. During the 2nd Wave the Six Sigma movement was extended to the lower levels of the organization. The performance from the 2nd Wave in the first half of 2004 was measured at about 149 billion Korean won through the improvement of network quality, decrease in service failure, and lead-time reduction. The Six Sigma movement in KT has evolved as it went though a series of Wave. When the 3rd Wave was completed, the high level executives became a part of the projects and the "lean" Six Sigma focusing on customer contact management was introduced. At the 5th Wave, many of the chosen projects were those involving multiple functions, implying that the Six Sigma movement started looking at work from process perspective. The process perspective was expanded to the upstream suppliers at the 6th Wave, helping them to adopt the Six Sigma initiative.

The Six Sigma initiative at KT has contributed not just to the financial performance but also to the competence development of human resources. As December 2007, over 8% of total employees were certified as having one of Master Black Belt (MBB), Black Belt (BB), Green Belt (GB). With this pool of human resources, KT can perform Six Sigma education and consulting without the help from outside experts (Figure 4).

|  | MBB | BB | GB | Total |
|---|---|---|---|---|
| No. of employees | 106 | 198 | 2,849 | 3,153 |
| % of total employees | 0.3% | 0.5% | 7.6% | 8.4% |

Fig. 4    Number of Certified Six Sigma Belt in KT.
*Source*: KT's CSR Reports (2008).

# 3  BPM (Business Process Management) in KT

## 3.1  *Background of BPM introduction*

Although the Six Sigma initiative in KT was successful and was applied widely throughout the company, KT encountered its limitation as it did before with other initiatives. When KT previously adopted TQC, BPR, and other new management programs, they failed to bring real business performance. Therefore, those programs had to be ceased. The Six Sigma initiative also ran into the similar problems.

Firstly, the Six Sigma program is a problem-solving method based on projects. However, the projects in KT were mostly at the low functional level with the orientation on small scale activities. Recognizing this problem, KT tried to find large scale projects; however, it did not work as hoped. Secondly, the Six Sigma program was not linked directly to the firm's strategic goals. Since the Six Sigma projects were not derived from KT's management goals, the project leaders did not have consistent criteria in choosing Critical To Quality (CTQ). The result was that the contribution from projects was very limited. Thirdly, KT had difficulties in identifying projects to be applied on a systematic and structural manner since the business processes were not clearly defined. Since the Six Sigma projects were not chosen from the perspective of process, it frequently happened that the selected projects were duplicated. Besides, the measurement system for performance and quality was not based on the process perspective. Fourthly, the system for continuous improvement was imperfect due to the absence of monitoring and execution tools for follow-up. Lastly, it was difficult to execute cross-functional tasks because of the barrier between functional departments which disturbed cooperation.

To deal with these problems, KT realized the need to perform all the management activities based on process approach, which led KT to adopt BPM in 2006. KT set the strategy and goal of providing high value to customers. To achieve the goal, the firm identified major processes, and then focused on improving those processes continuously to achieve maximum efficiency. KT realized two major problems at the time that BPM was introduced. First, most processes lacked the visibility because they were neither standardized nor digitalized. It was difficult to know which department performed a particular process, who actually performed a given process, and how long the lead-time for each process was. Therefore, it was unrealistic to expect any true improvement in the situation. The second problem was related to the IT system. As the databases of information systems were connected in a tightly coupled structure, they were not working independently. It implied that if a failure occurred anywhere in the link, its impact was not just on the failed system but on the other systems as well. Therefore, the IT system suffered from a lack of flexibility. To resolve these problems to the roots, KT decided that BPM is required in order to increase the visibility of processes and establish a flexible IT infrastructure.

## 3.2  *Strategy for BPM introduction*

KT chose the phase-in approach as the strategy for BPM introduction like in Figure 5. The first stage is to build a platform of BPM with a standardized IT infrastructure. The goal is to aggregate all the information occurring in each process and to make it available for any business unit that needs it. The second stage is to construct a methodology of applying BPM so that it functions well in KT's unique environment and to earn companywide consensus. The next step is to choose the first trial process that fits the BPM environment and can bring successful outcomes. Based on the experience of implementing BPM to the chosen process it is expected to develop a Business Process Management System (BPMS). The fourth stage is to establish a detailed action plan for extending BPM throughout the company and to build an integrated BPMS and a portal for BPM. The final stage is to realize a companywide total process management, through which KT can achieve its "Future Strategy 2010" to fortify its position as a global company.

KT expects a remarkable outcome from BPM in 2008, when the above stages are completed. Those quantifiable measures such as the amount of time to perform tasks, time to check the data for error, and time to do work communication will be reduced. As a consequence, productivity will be improved and profitability will also be improved noticeably. It is expected that the qualitative effect will be enormous as well. The visibility of processes will be enhanced, and the level of understanding works and

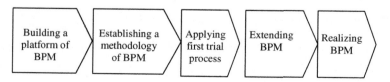

Fig. 5   The Stages for Introducing BPM in KT.

tasks will also be increased. In addition, the productivity will be improved due to the real time monitoring of the work progress. In the past when the organization was structured on the basis of functions, there were problems that works were overlapped and conflicted between functions so that work progresses were delayed. However, BPM is expected to shorten the lead time for works by streamlining the flow of work processes. Furthermore, it will be possible to understand in real time how the processes are progressing and what the performances are so that resolving errors and deficiency will be easier and faster than before.

## 4 Examples of Process Management in KT

Although KT is still at the early stage of the BPM, defining and improving works from the perspective of process has been long. In this section, we are going to present two actual cases about how KT defined and improved the work processes. KT categorized all the work performed in the firm into 10 processes as shown in Figure 6. In the past when work was organized based on function, errors and work delays occurred frequently and poor cooperation between functions were not rare. However, in the process of pursuing customer oriented management, KT redefined the work from the process perspective after analyzing their linkages and orders. Defining processes in such a way make it easy for the firm to understand work flows and support them with information technology. KT utilized these benefits to accelerate the movement of process innovation.

### 4.1 *New product (service) development process*

The competition in Korea telecommunication industry has been keen as the industry, previously under government-controlled monopoly, was open to private sector. After KT was privatized in 1998 and thus true competition began, KT has still been enjoying its dominant position in the market. However, businesses in long-distance call and super-speed internet are being chased by competitors very rapidly. Furthermore, since communication market is becoming increasingly globalized, the competition will be much keener in the future. To grow steadily in this competitive environment, KT recognized the need to continually develop new services for consumer needs. So, the company has focused its efforts to rebuild the new product development process and operate it efficiently. Figure 7 shows the new product development process that emphasizes customer orientation.

| Process | Range | Example |
|---|---|---|
| Strategic Planning | From reviewing long-term trend of market to short-term business planning | Company vision, Future forecasting, Business strategy |
| Customer Relationship Management | From identifying potential demand to attaining new customers | Customer classification, Demand Research, Responsive system |
| New Product Development | From identifying customers' needs to releasing new products | Product management, Product development, R&D |
| Order Processing | From creating new customers to terminating contract with customer | New contract, Contract renewal, Contract termination |
| Failure Resolving Process | From receiving failure reports to satisfying the customer | Receipt of failure reports, Examining, Repairing, Processing |
| Fee Management | From fee recognition to payment | Fee calculation, Charging, Receiving |
| Facility Operation | Maintenance/check and repair after acquiring facility | Transfer, Transmission, Operation/maintenance of lines |
| Communication Network Building | From researching demand for facility to building the network | Planning for communication network, Investment planning, Network building |
| Management Support | From identifying requirements for support to satisfying the requirements | Finance, Delivery, Human resource management |
| Interested Parties Management | From understanding needs to resolving the needs | Government, National assembly, Public opinion, Stockholders, Suppliers |

Fig. 6   Major Work Processes in KT.

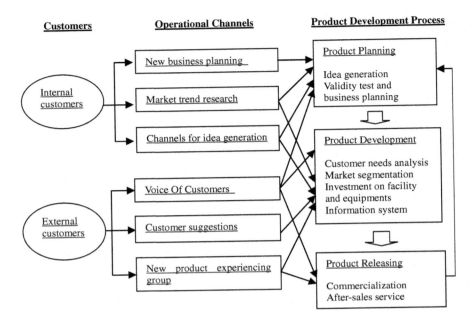

Fig. 7   The New Product Development Process in KT.

The new product development process consists of product planning, product development, and product releasing. At the product planning stage, ideas for new services are generated and their validities are tested. Then the idea that passes the procedure is formulated into the specific plan for business. Ideas for new services can be generated from all the possible channels including external customers' complaints or suggestions, internal customers' suggestions, new technology information from market trend analysis, and information about competitor's products. At the product development stage, the target market for the chosen product is specified and the needs from the target market are identified. Then the product is designed based on the identified needs. In addition, the facility and equipments needed for production are procured and the appropriate information system is built. The final stage is product releasing stage where the developed product is delivered to customers and after-sales services are performed.

KT also defined the sub-processes for each operational channel of new product development process shown in Figure 7. For example, for the market trend research process, KT defined a sub-process involving plan development, data collection, data analysis, and report write-up in order to systematically collect and analyze the trends related to competitors, technology, and customers. To acquire and analyze useful information easily, KT participates regularly in associations of communication specialists and operates marketing consultants group to capture the market trends. The Management Research Center inside KT also plays an important role for the research on business environments. In addition, KT assigns personnel in the key departments and subsidiary firms to the job of acquiring and analyzing market related information. KT circulates the reports on market trend regularly throughout the company and also shares the direction for future business and marketing issues within the company through monthly magazines.

## 4.2 *Financial accounting process*

The financial accounting process is one of the key processes for management supports, which manages the flow of financial assets. Information provided by this process is essential for top management to make decisions, therefore rapidly delivering of precise financial information is extremely important in the process. KT, as shown in Figure 8, defines the financial accounting process to consist of four sub- processes in sequence. As the starting sub-process, budget management process is to establish the overall plan about how to acquire and operate the financial resources. In other words, it is the process that determines the size of financial budget and allocates it to various uses. Next sub-process is the cash management process that establishes the detailed cash demand and supply plan and manages cash accounts such as deposits and installment savings

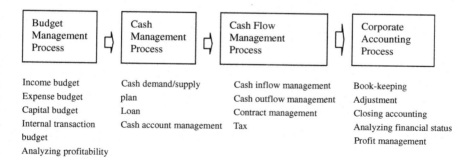

Fig. 8    Financial Accounting Process.

with the management of loan, corporate bond and securities as resources for cash. The following sub-process is a cash flow management process that approves and implements actual inflow and outflow of cash. The final sub-process is the corporate accounting process which is related to cost accounting and closing accounting. This process collects all the aspects of financial performance and then performs financial status and profitability analyses, which becomes a feedback into the next period's budgeting process. KT divided these four sub-processes into 32 detailed lower level processes and defined the work flow of each process. Furthermore, KT defined performance measures for each process through which KT regularly assesses its performance and identifies the opportunity for improvement.

## 5  Conclusion

According to a recent survey with 153 CEOs of the largest 1,000 firms in Korea, 87 percent of respondents have said that they are currently in the process of business innovation. This implies that almost all firms of today jump on the bandwagon of business innovation. One reason why it is so popular is that the environment surrounding firms is changing so rapidly that the firms feel they might be forced to retire from the market if they fail to adjust to the changing environment. According to the survey mentioned above, the innovation initiative that was mentioned the most by the surveyed CEOs is Customer Satisfaction Management followed by Process Innovation. This mirrors the reality that firms raise their concern on process, which is somewhat influenced by BPR and BPM. We can see a variety of goals set by firms such as customer satisfaction, profit maximization, or enhanced competitiveness, and so forth. However, no matter what the goal is, the tool for achieving the goal should be based on the process. How effectively the process is designed and how efficiently it is operated are the keys to achieving the goal. Therefore, process innovation will continue to receive high attention from companies and studies on process innovation methodology will continue.

In this research, we studied how KT, a representative communication firm in Korea, introduced BPM and what strategy it applied in applying BPM. KT was established as a public company however, its privatization process began in 1998 and completed in 2002 as the shares owned by the Korean government was completely sold. The communication market also changed to a free competition market by opening its door to domestic and international firms. Faced with these environment changes, KT continually adopted many initiatives for business innovation in order to retain and reinforce its competitiveness. KT introduced BPM as one of its series of strategic choices. As a method for introducing BPM, KT chose a stage-by-stage method. Currently, KT is at the beginning stage of its introduction and is in the process of linking it with IT infra-structure. By 2008 when BPM is settled down, it is expected that the competitiveness of KT will be elevated dramatically.

## References

Champy, J.A. (2002). *X-Engineering the Corporation*, Warner Books.

Chang, J.F. (2005). *Business Process Management Systems: Strategy and Implementation.* Auerbach Publications.

Hammer, M. and J.A. Champy (1993). *Reengineering the Corporation: A Manifesto for Business Revolution*, HarperCollins Publishers Ltd.

Hammer, M. (2002). Process Management and the Future of Six Sigma, *Sloan Management Review*, 43(2), pp. 26–33.

Harrington, H.J. (1997). *Business Process Improvement*, McGraw-Hill.

Smith, H. and P. Fingar (2003). *Business Process Management: The Third Wave*, Meghan-Kiffer Press.

Smith, R.F. (2006). *Business Process Management and Balanced Scorecard: Focusing Processes on Strategic Drivers.* Wiley.

Tenner, A.R. and I.J. Detoro (2000). *Process Redesign: The Implementation Guide for Managers*, Prentice Hall.

# PART 3

# EMPIRICAL STUDIES OF BPM IN JAPANESE AND KOREAN COMPANIES

# 9

# Current Status of Process Management in Japanese and Korean Companies

Keisuke Sakate
*Osaka University of Commerce, Japan*

Naoya Yamaguchi
*Niigata University, Japan*

## 1  Introduction

Information assets are becoming a means of obtaining competitive advantage, and it has become crucial to attain new methods of utilizing and managing these assets. As a result of increased competition, the commercial initiative has shifted from suppliers to customers, and an appropriate response by suppliers — one that will ensure customer satisfaction — is now a critical means of securing competitive advantage.

Interdivisional cooperation is necessary in responding to customer power, as is interorganizational business process management that promotes interdivisional cooperation. Conventional management accounting has focused on an evaluation system for the vertically segmented organization, but it is now necessary to adopt the viewpoint of Process Based Management, which (i) emphasizes the process as the axis of performance evaluation, (ii) is concerned with interprocess coordination, whether intra- or extra-firm, and (iii) places the emphasis on this core process.

This study presents the results of an actual condition survey of process management, undertaken in 2004, which focused in particular on the relationships between process innovation and certain factors (customer participation and competitive factors) in Japanese and Korean companies.

## 2 The Framework of Analysis of This Study and a Brief Summary of Enterprise Investigation

### 2.1 *The framework of analysis*

The analytic framework used in this paper is part of the conceptual framework of the actual condition survey, which was conducted by the Strategic Process Management Expert Committee (where Gunyung Lee is the chairman). This committee was established to undertake enterprise investigation projects.

Figure 1 shows the focus of this paper. The study shows how the participation of customers of the inside or outside companies, IT tools for process management, and competitive elements influenced innovative changes in the business process.

### 2.2 *Brief summary of Japanese and Korean enterprise investigation*

To investigate Japanese enterprises, we sent questionnaires to 1281 manufacturing companies (including 973 listed or over-the-counter and 308 unlisted companies), based on "Companies' List of Personnel", published

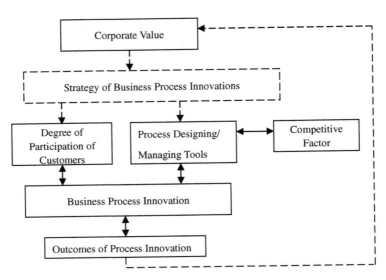

Fig. 1   Framework of the Survey.

in 2003 by Diamond Inc. The questionnaires were sent on 1 March 2004, and the closing date was 30 March 2004. We received 198 answers, of which 193 were valid responses.

Meanwhile, to investigate Korean enterprises, we sent questionnaires to 515 listed companies and 312 manufacturing companies listed on Korean Securities Dealers Automated Quotations (KOSDAQ). In addition, we interviewed some companies. We received answers to questionnaires from 105 companies, of which 100 responses were valid. The questionnaires had been sent and collected from February to May 2004.

## 2.3 *Outline of responded companies*

Figure 2 shows the types of business of the responding companies. In Japan, the appliance and electrical equipments industry accounted for the highest percentage of responses with 35 companies forming 18.1%, followed by petroleum, chemical and rubber industry, machinery, precision instruments industry and food and groceries industry.

In Korea, the food and groceries industry accounted for the highest percentage of respondents with 18 companies (18.0%), followed by

|  | Japan | | Korea | |
|---|---|---|---|---|
|  | Number | Ratio (%) | Number | Ratio (%) |
| Appliance and Electrical Equipments | 35 | 18.1 | 13 | 13.0 |
| Petroleum, Chemical and Rubber | 32 | 16.6 | 12 | 12.0 |
| Machinery and Precision Instruments | 28 | 14.5 | 4 | 4.0 |
| Food and Groceries | 23 | 11.9 | 18 | 18.0 |
| Equipments for Transportation | 11 | 5.7 | 14 | 14.0 |
| Textile Fabrics | 7 | 3.6 | 4 | 4.0 |
| Papers and Pulp | 4 | 2.1 | 2 | 2.0 |
| Medicaments | 6 | 3.1 | 5 | 5.0 |
| Steel, Metal, Metalloids | 16 | 8.3 | 9 | 9.0 |
| Glasses and Mineral Products | 3 | 1.6 | 1 | 1.0 |
| Others | 18 | 9.3 | 17 | 17.0 |
| Blank (no response) | 10 | 5.2 | 1 | 1.0 |
| Total | 193 | 100% | 100 | 100% |

Fig. 2   Types of Businesses of Respondents.

transportation equipment, electrical appliances and equipment, and the oil, chemical, and rubber industry.

In this survey, we combined the use of questions by categories, and employed 5-point Likert Scale questions. In this paper, we illustrate the features of the process management of Japanese and Korean companies by cross-tabulation and assess the significance of the relationship between the effects of environmental change and the intervening variable on process management, using chi-square analysis. For chi-square analysis, we used the exact probability test (Monte Carlo, 95 percent confidence level).

## 3 Result of Positive Analysis

### 3.1 *Production, management and competitive environment in Japan and Korean companies*

Figure 3 shows the cross-tabulation form of production and planning for production of the responding companies. In terms of production planning, in both Japan and Korea, a large majority of companies adopted a mixture of job-order and stock production.

| Production Planning \ Production form | Small-lot | Medium-lot | Mass | Other | Total |
|---|---|---|---|---|---|
| **Japan** | | | | | |
| Job-order | **29 (16.1)** | 19 (10.6) | 14 (7.8) | 0 (0.0) | 62 (34.4) |
| Stock | 5 (2.8) | 14 (7.8) | **29 (16.1)** | 0 (0.0) | 48 (26.7) |
| Mixture | 25 (13.9) | **28 (15.6)** | 16 (8.9) | 0 (0.0) | 73 (38.3) |
| Others | 0 (0.0) | 0 (0.0) | 1 (0.6) | 0 (0.0) | 1 (0.6) |
| Total | 60 (32.8) | 61 (33.9) | 60 (33.3) | 0 (0.0) | 180 (100) |
| **Korea** | | | | | |
| Job-order | 10 (10.0) | 3 (3.0) | **14 (14.0)** | 0 (0.0) | 27 (27.0) |
| Stock | 1 (1.0) | 7 (7.0) | **18 (18.0)** | 0 (0.0) | 26 (26.0) |
| Mixture | 5 (5.0) | 10 (10.0) | **28 (28.0)** | 0 (0.0) | 43 (43.0) |
| Others | 1 (1.0) | 0 (0.0) | 0 (0.0) | 3 (3.0) | 4 (4.0) |
| Total | 17 (17.0) | 20 (20.0) | 60 (60.0) | 3 (3.0) | 100 (100) |

(The numbers in parentheses represent the percent of respondents)

Fig. 3   Kind of Production and Production Planning of Responded Companies.

| | Japan | | Korea | |
|---|---|---|---|---|
| | Last 5 Years | Next 5 Years | Last 5 Years | Next 5 Years |
| Price | **129 (69.7)** | **102 (55.7)** | **62 (62.6)** | **45 (45.5)** |
| Quality | 36 (19.5) | **47 (25.7)** | 25 (25.2) | **31 (31.3)** |
| Delivery time | 2 (1.1) | 1 (0.5) | 2 (2.0) | 2 (2.0) |
| New products release | 16 (8.6) | **27 (14.8)** | 5 (5.1) | **10 (10.1)** |
| After-sales service | 1 (0.5) | 2 (1.1) | 1 (1.0) | 2 (2.0) |
| Ecology | 0 (0.0) | 3 (1.6) | 1 (1.0) | 4 (4.0) |
| Product design | 1 (0.5) | 1 (0.5) | 2 (2.0) | 4 (4.0) |
| Others | — | — | 1 (1.0) | 1 (1.0) |
| Total | 185 (100) | 183 (100) | 99 (100) | 99 (100) |

(The numbers in parentheses represent percents of respondents)

Fig. 4    Hardest Part of Competition.

There was a significant difference between Japan and Korea in the forms of production. In Japan, all forms showed about the same rate, whereas mass production accounted for 60% of all production by the Korean companies that responded.

We asked the companies what the most difficult part of competition had been in the last five years, and what it would be in the next five years. Figure 4 shows the results. Both Japanese and Korean companies considered price as the most difficult aspect of competition in the last five years, and they believed that this trend would continue in the next five years. However, the number of companies that considered "price" as an aspect of difficulty decreased from 129 (69.7%) to 102 (55.7%) in Japan, and from 62 (62.6%) to 45 (45.5%) in Korea. On the other hand, the number of companies that considered quality and new products released as the most difficult parts increased.

## 3.2    *Process innovation and informatization*

Figures 5A and 5B show spreadsheets of the degree of process innovation in Japan and Korea in the last five years. We used 4-level answers for Japanese companies but 3-level answers for Korean companies. We did not offer the choice of "sales" in the questionnaire sent to Japanese companies. The spreadsheets enable us to draw the analysis that both Japanese and Korean companies have attempted not only to enhance their supply chain, but also to improve their production process.

|  | Innovation | | | | |
|  | Company-wide | Partial | Improve | Remain | Ave. |
|---|---|---|---|---|---|
| Buy in process | **18 (9.3)** | 71 (36.8) | 57 (29.5) | 39 (20.2) | 2.37 |
| R&D process | 10 (5.2) | 67 (34.7) | 57 (29.5) | 47 (24.4) | 2.22 |
| Production | 12 (6.2) | 90 (46.6) | 53 (27.5) | 31 (16.1) | 2.45 |
| Inventory management | **15 (7.8)** | 58 (30.1) | 55 (28.5) | 57 (29.5) | 2.17 |
| Distribution | **22 (11.4)** | 56 (29.0) | 59 (30.6) | 49 (25.4) | 2.26 |
| After-sales service | 3 (1.6) | 38 (19.7) | 61 (31.6) | 80 (41.5) | 1.80 |
| Management | 10 (5.2) | 60 (31.1) | 71 (36.8) | 44 (22.8) | 2.19 |
| Cooperation with abroad | 6 (3.1) | 44 (22.8) | 48 (24.9) | 75 (38.9) | 1.89 |
| Recycle | 11 (5.7) | 57 (29.5) | 69 (35.8) | 49 (25.4) | 2.16 |

(The numbers in parentheses represent percents of respondents)

Fig. 5A    Degree of Process Innovation in Japan.

|  | Innovation | Improvement | Remain | Ave. |
|---|---|---|---|---|
| Buy in process | **25 (25.0)** | 64 (64.0) | 9 (9.0) | 2.16 |
| R&D process | 15 (15.0) | 66 (66.0) | 17 (17.0) | 1.98 |
| Production | 24 (24.0) | 62 (62.0) | 11 (11.0) | 2.13 |
| Inventory management | **25 (25.0)** | 56 (56.0) | 16 (16.0) | 2.09 |
| Distribution | **26 (26.0)** | 56 (56.0) | 15 (15.0) | 2.11 |
| After-sales service | 13 (13.0) | 69 (69.0) | 15 (15.0) | 1.98 |
| Management | 19 (19.0) | 60 (60.0) | 18 (18.0) | 2.01 |
| Cooperation with abroad | 9 (9.0) | 53 (53.0) | 34 (34.0) | 1.74 |
| Recycle | 6 (6.0) | 62 (62.0) | 28 (28.0) | 1.77 |
| Sales | 17 (17.0) | 63 (63.0) | 17 (17.0) | 2.00 |

(The numbers in parentheses represent percents of respondents)

Fig. 5B    Degree of Process Innovation in Korea.

We also suggest that, in addition to enhancing the supply chain, many Japanese companies have also undertaken an innovation of the R&D process, and that Korean companies have undertaken an innovation in the downstream of the supply chain, such as sales and after-sales service.

We then asked a question about relations with customers and business process innovation in the last five years. The answers to this question were measured on five-point scales (5: completely YES to 1: completely NO). The results are shown in Figure 6. We found that, in both companies, customer demands had been introduced into the process, or that several units

| Last 5 Years | Japan | Korea |
|---|---|---|
| Introduce customers demands into process | **3.97** | **3.92** |
| Customers are concerned in process innovation | 2.65 | 3.33 |
| Suppliers and partners are concerned in process innovation | 2.81 | 3.36 |
| Customers are concerned about developing new products | **3.48** | **3.54** |
| Several units in the company work in cooperation with in order to innovate processes | **3.85** | **3.96** |
| Suppliers and partners are concerned about developing new products | 3.02 | 3.38 |

Fig. 6   Degree of Customers' Participation of Customers in Process Innovation (average).

in the company now worked in cooperation with customers to innovate processes, or that customers had participated in developing new products. We also presume that, in both Japan and Korea, units in the company took charge of process innovation, while customers played an important part in the concrete definition and design of the process.

We also asked several questions to establish the trend of informatization in the responding companies. First, we asked them to choose one out of three options regarding the objectives of IT investment. The results are shown in Figure 7. In Japan, the highest trend, both for the last five years and for the next five, is the "speed-up of operation". However, the proportion that gave this response decreased. In Korea, the highest trend for the last five years has been the "speed-up of operation". But "improvement of customer satisfaction" now seems to be the most important. Meanwhile, Japanese companies emphasized the "reduction of inventory cost", while Korean companies emphasized "improvement of development capability of new product or service". This trend indicates that Korean companies want to utilize IT to improve their customer relationships.

Next, we asked a question about the utilization of IT tools. The results are shown in Figure 8. For the category of "Already Introduced", both Japan and South Korea reflect their responses in the following order: ERP (Enterprise Resource Planning), Knowledge Management, SCM (Supply Chain Management), Data Management, and CRM (Customer Relationship Management). Moreover, adding the category of "Will Be Introduced in the Next 5 Years", while Japanese companies are ranked: ERP, Knowledge Management, Data Management, SCM and CRM, Korean Companies are ranked: ERP, the knowledge Management, Data

|  | Japan | | Korea | |
|---|---|---|---|---|
|  | Last 5 Years | Next 5 Years | Last 5 Years | Next 5 Years |
| Reduction of inventory cost | 51 (26.4) | 57 (29.5) | 36 (36.0) | 19 (19.0) |
| Reduction of procurement cost | 27 (14.0) | 68 (35.2) | 14 (14.0) | 13 (13.0) |
| Reduction of personnel expenses | 61 (31.6) | 38 (19.7) | 33 (33.0) | 19 (19.0) |
| Speed-up of operation | 156 (80.8) | 106 (54.9) | 61 (61.0) | 50 (50.0) |
| Reinforcement of sales force | 81 (42.0) | 78 (40.4) | 30 (30.0) | 34 (34.0) |
| Improvement of development capability of new product or service | 30 (15.5) | 21 (10.9) | 18 (18.0) | 37 (37.0) |
| Increase of client/business partner or reinforcement of business partnership | 20 (10.4) | 23 (11.9) | 9 (9.0) | 17 (17.0) |
| Improvement of customer satisfaction | 39 (20.2) | 90 (46.6) | 24 (24.0) | 53 (53.0) |
| New entry to other business area | 3 (1.6) | 10 (5.2) | 3 (3.0) | 7 (7.0) |
| Organizational revolution like efficiency improvement | 58 (30.1) | 48 (24.9) | 49 (49.0) | 38 (38.0) |
| Other | 5 (2.6) | 5 (2.6) | 3 (3.0) | 2 (2.0) |

(The numbers in parentheses represent percents of respondents)

Fig. 7    Objective of IT Investment.

|  | Already Introduced | | Will Be Introduced in the Next 5 Years | | No Schedule | |
|---|---|---|---|---|---|---|
|  | Japan | Korea | Japan | Korea | Japan | Korea |
| CRM | 23 (11.9) | 29 (29.0) | 69 (35.8) | 49 (49.0) | 94 (48.7) | 16 (16.0) |
| Knowledge Management | 32 (16.6) | 40 (40.0) | 76 (39.4) | 45 (45.0) | 75 (38.9) | 9 (9.0) |
| Data Management | 29 (15.0) | 35 (35.0) | 74 (38.3) | 47 (47.0) | 82 (42.5) | 14 (14.0) |
| ERP | 45 (23.3) | 61 (61.0) | 77 (39.9) | 37 (37.0) | 64 (33.2) | 2 (2.0) |
| SCM | 32 (16.6) | 35 (35.0) | 68 (35.2) | 42 (42.0) | 84 (43.5) | 16 (16.0) |

(The numbers in parentheses represent percents of respondents)

Fig. 8    Utilization of IT Tools.

Management, CRM and SCM. In addition, as an overall view of "Already Introduced" and "Will Be Introduced in the Next 5 Years" catogories, the ratio of Korean companies is higher than Japanese companies. Therefore, we presume that Korean companies actively use the IT tools.

## 4  Verification of Causal Relationships Between Process Innovation and Some Factors

### 4.1  *Causal relationships between process innovation and customers' participation*

Figures 9A and 9B show the result of chi-square analysis between process innovation and participation by related business units. The numbers in cells represent the significance probability (both sides significance probability of Monte Carlo simulation), and the colored cells mean 95% confidence level. There was a significant difference between Japan and Korea in "Buy in process".

Korean companies that concentrate on the innovation of *buy in process* would reflect customers' demands in its internal process — several units would work in cooperation with process innovation, and its customers would be concerned about developing new products.

On the other side, there was no specially significant relationship in Japan. In addition, for cooperation with abroad process in Japan, if companies concentrate on the process, both inside and outside related business units would be deeply concerned about process innovation, but in South Korea, there would be only several inside units in the company that would work in cooperation.

### 4.2  *Causal relationships between process innovation and competitive factor*

Figures 10A and 10B show the result of chi-square analysis between process innovation and the hardest part of competition in the past five years.

There was a significant difference between Japan and Korea in the kind of process innovation that companies which considered quality as the most difficult aspect of competition would concentrate on. In Japan, they would concentrate on research and development, production, and cooperation with abroad. But, in Korea, they would concentrate on buy in process, inventory management, and distribution. In addition, because there was no company which answered the environment protection as the most difficult aspect of competition, chi-square analysis for its factor could not be done.

In Japan, there were several significant relationships between companies which considered new product release as the most difficult aspect of competition and process innovation (production, after-sales service,

| | Introduce Customers Demands into Process Innovation | Customers are Concerned in Process Innovation | Suppliers and Partners are Concerned in Process Innovation | Customers are Concerned in Developing New Products | Several Units Work in Cooperation with Process Innovation | Suppliers and Partners are Concerned in Developing New Products |
|---|---|---|---|---|---|---|
| Buy in process | .980 | .176 | .135 | .736 | .052 | .539 |
| R&D process | .689 | .342 | .254 | .487 | .171 | .166 |
| Production | .036 | .244 | .358 | .979 | .005 | .710 |
| Inventory management | .57 | .446 | .440 | .907 | .446 | .850 |
| Distribution | .539 | .010 | .016 | .767 | .751 | .285 |
| After-sales service | .725 | .570 | .275 | .850 | .736 | .078 |
| Management | .466 | .959 | .518 | .953 | .404 | .860 |
| Cooperation with abroad | .995 | .023 | .017 | .829 | .969 | .029 |
| Recycle | .648 | .347 | .347 | .466 | .098 | .528 |

Fig. 9A   Causal Relationships between Process Innovation and Customers' Participation (Japanese Companies).

| | Introduce Customers Demands into Process Innovation | Customers are Concerned in Process Innovation | Suppliers and Partners are Concerned in Process Innovation | Customers are Concerned in Developing New Products | Several Units Work in Cooperation with Process Innovation | Suppliers and Partners are Concerned in Developing New Products |
|---|---|---|---|---|---|---|
| Buy in process | .010 | .156 | .072 | .083 | .000 | .021 |
| R&D process | .177 | .813 | .719 | .000 | .093 | .010 |
| Production | .042 | .469 | .250 | .323 | .010 | .563 |
| Inventory management | .010 | .208 | .167 | .771 | .083 | .479 |
| Distribution | .074 | .458 | .677 | .875 | .021 | .385 |
| After-sales service | .000 | .646 | .344 | .147 | .063 | .208 |
| Management | .365 | .656 | .844 | .615 | .010 | .698 |
| Cooperation with abroad | .074 | .177 | .095 | .085 | .011 | .385 |
| Recycle | .333 | .137 | .116 | .417 | .406 | .167 |

Fig. 9B   Causal Relationships between Process Innovation and Customers' Participation (Korean Companies).

| | Price | Quality | Delivery Time | New Product Release | After-sales Service | Ecology | Design |
|---|---|---|---|---|---|---|---|
| Buy in process | .514 | .729 | .298 | .497 | .641 | — | 1.000 |
| R&D process | .420 | .023 | 1.000 | .166 | 1.000 | — | .657 |
| Production | .006 | .006 | .525 | .006 | 1.000 | — | 1.000 |
| Inventory management | .707 | .221 | .580 | .442 | .376 | — | .086 |
| Distribution | .265 | .442 | 1.000 | .448 | .348 | — | .123 |
| After-sales service | .580 | .160 | 1.000 | .000 | .210 | — | .530 |
| Management | .094 | .785 | .105 | .066 | 1.000 | — | .591 |
| Cooperation with abroad | .381 | .036 | .541 | .000 | 1.000 | — | 1.000 |
| Recycle | .481 | .331 | 1.000 | .381 | 1.000 | — | 1.000 |

Fig. 10A   Causal Relationships between Process Innovation and Hardest Part of Competition (Japanese Companies).

| | Price | Quality | Delivery Time | New Product Release | After-sales Service | Ecology | Design |
|---|---|---|---|---|---|---|---|
| Buy in process | .071 | .010 | 1.000 | 1.000 | 1.000 | .112 | .680 |
| R&D process | .577 | .825 | .309 | .691 | .392 | 1.000 | 1.000 |
| Production | .392 | .495 | .082 | .845 | .381 | 1.000 | .742 |
| Inventory management | .196 | .010 | .093 | .629 | .237 | .237 | 1.000 |
| Distribution | .268 | .000 | 1.000 | .113 | .206 | .206 | 1.000 |
| After-sales service | 1.000 | .619 | 1.000 | .649 | 1.000 | .299 | 1.000 |
| Management | .649 | .876 | .093 | .186 | .485 | .268 | 1.000 |
| Cooperation with abroad | .063 | .454 | .649 | .227 | 1.000 | 1.000 | .649 |
| Recycle | .979 | .732 | .649 | .753 | .402 | .402 | .649 |

Fig. 10B   Causal Relationships between Process Innovation and Hardest Part of Competition (Korean Companies).

management, and cooperation with abroad). But in Korea, there were several significant relationships between companies which considered quality as the most difficult aspect of competition and process innovation (buy-in process, inventory management, and distribution).

## 4.3 Causal relationships between process innovation and introduction of IT tools

Figures 11A and 11B show the result of chi-square analysis between process innovation and introduction of IT tools.

Between Japanese and Korean companies, were some common IT tools like Data Management and SCM which had closely relations with process innovation. But there were some differences between both countries in some other IT tools like Knowledge Management and ERP. For Knowledge Management, it had a significant relation with only one process (management) in Japan, but in Korea, it had significant relations with four processes (buy in process, inventory management, distribution, and after-sales service). In addition, ERP had a significant relation with management process only in Korea, but it had significant relations with seven processes in Japan.

There were some differences between both countries the IT tools which companies introduce for process innovation. But a more detailed analysis is needed to understand the reason of such differences.

| | CRM | Knowledge Management | Data Management | ERP | SCM |
|---|---|---|---|---|---|
| Buy in process | .088 | .873 | .039 | .000 | .017 |
| R&D process | .056 | .464 | .149 | .392 | .254 |
| Production | .365 | .481 | .525 | .038 | .227 |
| Inventory management | .039 | .978 | .530 | .039 | .011 |
| Distribution | .000 | .381 | .049 | .000 | .000 |
| After-sales service | .000 | .304 | .011 | .376 | .006 |
| Management | .016 | .017 | .370 | .005 | .017 |
| Cooperation with abroad | .685 | .967 | .018 | .035 | .663 |
| Recycle | .044 | .409 | .155 | .011 | .000 |

Fig. 11A   Causal Relationships between Process Innovation and Introduction of IT Tools (Japanese Companies).

| | CRM | Knowledge Management | Data Management | ERP | SCM |
|---|---|---|---|---|---|
| Buy in process | .000 | .032 | .000 | .347 | .000 |
| R&D process | .473 | .196 | .063 | .082 | .000 |
| Production | .086 | .054 | .126 | .072 | .043 |
| Inventory management | .301 | .022 | .032 | .175 | .000 |
| Distribution | .462 | .033 | .043 | .113 | .000 |
| After-sales service | .022 | .011 | .000 | .938 | .478 |
| Management | .183 | .172 | .084 | .000 | .000 |
| Cooperation with abroad | .581 | .054 | .979 | .542 | .165 |
| Recycle | .022 | .348 | .468 | .260 | .264 |

Fig. 11B    Causal Relationships between Process Innovation and Introduction of IT Tools (Korean companies).

## 5  Conclusion

We analyzed various factors (inside business units' and customers' participation, process management tools, and competitive factors) which had some relationships with process innovation in Japan and Korea. According to the result, we concluded that the emphasis of process innovation was different in the two countries. While Japanese companies tend to focus on efficiency improvement of internal process, Korean companies tend to focus on efficiency improvement of input resources which they buy from outside.

A more detailed analysis is needed. But we have clarified in this paper that the process management would function as an effective way to improve a company's corporate value.

## References

Lee, G.Y. (2003). Business Process Redesign and Performance Management, in *Organizational Structure and Management Accounting*. (in Japanese) Edited by Monden, Y., Zeimukeiri-kyokai, pp. 207–229.

Lee, G.Y., M. Kosuga and Y. Nagasaka. (2006). *Strategic Process Management — Theory and Practice-*, Zeimukeiri-kyokai. (In Japanese)

Monden, Y. and G.Y. Lee. (2005). Conceptual Framework of Process Management and Management Accounting (in Japanese) *Kigyo-kaikei*, 57(5), pp. 18–25.

Nagasaka, Y. and K. Sakate. (2005). Analysis of Process Management of Japanese Companies (in Japanese) *Kigyo-kaikei*, 57(5), pp. 33–41.

Sakate, K., Yamaguchi, N., Nagasaka, Y. and G.Y. Lee. (2006). Process Management of Japanese and Korean Enterprise — An Investigation Model and Positive Analysis of the Company Actual Situation (in Japanese) *Kaikei*, 170(5), pp. 98–112.

# 10

# Comparison Between Japanese and Korean Companies from the Viewpoint of Balanced Scorecard

Yoshiyuki Nagasaka
*Konan University, Japan*

## 1 Introduction

Based on the survey results of Japanese and Korean companies regarding BPM (Monden and Lee, 2005), this paper focuses on the relationship between the degree of process reform and its outcomes. Categorical regression analysis with the framework of the Balanced Scorecard (BSC) (Kaplan and Norton, 1992) has been performed and the causal relationship between the effects and the degree of process reform is verified.

The strategic objectives and performance evaluation indexes should be diverse depending on the organization of companies in BSC laying a strategy in the core. However, the diversity of strategic objectives and performance evaluation indexes depends on the business processes in BSC laying business processes in the core. If a method of business process management is similar, there is a common point to objectives on the basis of a viewpoint of BSC and performance evaluation indexes. Here, based on such a viewpoint, similarities and differences between Japanese and Korean companies are discussed.

## 2 BPM and Diversity of Objectives of Strategy and Performance Evaluation Indexes

BSC has objectives and performance evaluation indexes from four viewpoints of "finance", "customer", "process" and "learning and growth" as the result of breakthrough of a vision and a strategy. An important characteristic of BSC is in three points of "linkage with a strategy and a performance evaluation index", "cause-and-effect relationships" and "performance drivers" (Kaplan and Norton, 1996). BSC replaces a strategy with objectives in four viewpoints to performance evaluation indexes, and these make causation clear between objectives and performance evaluation indexes. Causation between a performance evaluation index and a performance driver should be clear; then it can be evaluated how a strategic objective of a scheme was achieved and how strategic management is supported by all members' participation. As mentioned, BSC is positioned as a tool for strategy implementation. If a strategy for a scheme is not clear, process-based BSC is useful. Because, process improvement and process changes are considered by the causation between performance evaluation indexes and performance. Furthermore, the development of the process-based BSC can contribute to the strategy formation and practice of the strategy.

Mintzberg (1978) distinguished between strategy practice and strategy formulation in his paper "Patterns in Strategy Formation". Actually, both the realized strategy and the not-realized strategy exist in "Intended Strategy". The realized strategy is constructed with "Deliberate Strategy" and "Emergent Strategy". "Deliberate Strategy" is to be performed completely. "Emergent Strategy" is the strategy that was not intended at first, but was performed as a result.

The process-based BSC can create the "Emergent Strategy" and contribute to the formation of the whole strategy because the BSC has a function of the basis of strategic learning in the scheme in which the strategy is not clarified. Because the strategy depends on the outside environment and management resources for the scheme, the strategic objectives and performance evaluation indexes are diverse.

However, the diversity of objectives of the strategy and strategic performance evaluation indexes is dependent on diversity of the business process management and the processes themselves. If there are any common points in the business process management, there must be some common points in the objectives of the strategy and strategic performance evaluation indexes.

## 3   Analysis Method

A survey was conducted on Japanese and Korean companies and their BPM (Monden and Lee, 2005) with regard to eight areas — (1) Outline of company, (2) Environment inside of company, (3) Environment outside of company, (4) Adoption of new information technology, (5) customer relationship, (6) Relation between business environment and organization, (7) Business process strategy, and (8) Globalization of business process — A questionnaire was sent to 1,282 Japanese manufacturers and 827 Korean manufacturers from February to May 2004. 198 Japanese companies and 105 Korean ones responded to this survey. Questions by both five points Likert scale and categories were applied.

In this paper, the significance of the degree of business process management reform in Japanese and Korean enterprise and the connection with the results are inspected using a chi-square test. Correct probability test (Monte Carlo confidence level 95%) is applied as a chi-square test here. The outcomes of business process innovation have been examined based on the BSC framework (the Balanced Scorecard). Namely, categorical regression analysis was applied to investigate the causal relationship among the satisfied items of four groups: financial, customer, inner process and learning & growth. The item with the biggest contribution ratio for satisfied items using the correlation coefficient is analyzed.

As a result of categorical regression analysis, we can judge that there is a clear correlation if multiple correlation coefficients are high, and it is said that the contribution of the category is big if the coefficient of the standardization coefficient is high.

## 4   Business Process Innovation and Result

Business process management is a management technique that can improve enterprise value by reducing the distance between business processes and raising the productivity of the processes. Here, it does not make sense if the results of process innovation cannot be reverted to the enterprise value enhancement. How the result of process reform links enterprise performance evaluation is investigated here.

### 4.1   *Business process reform and performance evaluation*

According to the changes of management atmosphere, each company should have a structure that can improve business processes continuously. Here, the performance evaluation index for each process was investigated for Japanese and Korean enterprises. And, contents of the index were also asked about for Japanese enterprises.

| Process | Japanese Enterprises (193) | | | | | Korean Enterprises (100) | |
|---|---|---|---|---|---|---|---|
| | Index Exists | Index | | | Index Does Not Exist | Index Exists | Index Does Not Exist |
| | | Cost | Quality | Time | | | |
| Procurement | 120 (62%) | 106 | 28 | 8 | 64 (33%) | 72 (72%) | 20 (20%) |
| R&D | 94 (49%) | 24 | 53 | 40 | 88 (46%) | 67 (67%) | 25 (25%) |
| Manufacturing | 125 (65%) | 89 | 65 | 46 | 57 (30%) | 80 (80%) | 12 (12%) |
| Warehouse management | 95 (49%) | 70 | 15 | 16 | 84 (44%) | 59 (59%) | 33 (33%) |
| Physical distribution | 99 (51%) | 81 | 10 | 29 | 80 (41%) | 64 (64%) | 27 (27%) |
| Sales and after service | 61 (32%) | 18 | 39 | 14 | 115 (60%) | 63 (63%) | 27 (27%) |
| Administration | 69 (36%) | 34 | 20 | 24 | 111 (58%) | 61 (61%) | 30 (30%) |
| Alliance | 34 (18%) | 21 | 15 | 6 | 142 (74%) | 25 (25%) | 64 (64%) |
| Recycle | 57 (30%) | 40 | 17 | 2 | 120 (62%) | 31 (31%) | 59 (59%) |

Fig. 1   Performance Evaluation Index for Each Process.

The results are shown in Figure 1. The Japanese and Korean enterprises that replied that the performance evaluation index is set with procurement and production processes exceeds 60%. About 50% of Japanese enterprises have a performance evaluation index for the warehouse management process, physical distribution process and R&D process. But, the percentage in other processes is low. For example, it was only 36% in the administration process. The enterprises that have a performance evaluation index for indirect division were quite few. On the other hand, about 60% of Korean companies have performance evaluation indexes for administration process, physical distribution process, warehouse management process, R&D process, procurement process, production process, after-sales service process and administration process. It is said that more Korean companies have performance evaluation indexes than Japanese companies. In addition, in many Japanese enterprises the important performance evaluation index is cost for the procurement process, but the important indexes are quality and time as well as the cost for the manufacturing process.

## 4.2   *Satisfaction degree of process reform*

Figure 2 shows satisfaction degree of the effect of business process reform based on four viewpoints of BSC.

| Japanese Enterprise | Item | Satisfaction Degree | | | | | | Average of Each Group |
|---|---|---|---|---|---|---|---|---|
| | | 5 | 4 | 3 | 2 | 1 | Average | |
| Financial | Sales | 8 | 41 | 69 | 35 | 26 | 2.83 | 3.00 |
| | Cost effectiveness | 5 | 35 | 97 | 34 | 11 | 2.94 | |
| | Selling cost | 2 | 39 | 92 | 40 | 10 | 2.91 | |
| | General and administrative expenses | 6 | 45 | 79 | 43 | 10 | 2.97 | |
| | Production cost | 11 | 92 | 43 | 26 | 12 | 3.35 | |
| Customer | Customer satisfaction | 5 | 67 | 86 | 19 | 6 | 3.25 | 3.07 |
| | Market share | 3 | 37 | 97 | 35 | 11 | 2.92 | |
| | Customer fixing rate | 0 | 38 | 119 | 18 | 6 | 3.04 | |
| Internal process | Cycle time | 5 | 64 | 74 | 29 | 8 | 3.16 | 3.02 |
| | Return rate and claim | 4 | 3 | 88 | 45 | 10 | 2.64 | |
| | Ratio to keep appointed date of delivery | 11 | 65 | 79 | 24 | 5 | 3.29 | |
| | Quantity of inventory | 10 | 65 | 57 | 39 | 11 | 3.13 | |
| | Productivity of indirect section | 4 | 39 | 73 | 49 | 11 | 2.86 | |
| Learning and growth | Awareness of employees for changes | 5 | 60 | 83 | 22 | 13 | 3.12 | 3.05 |
| | Paradigm and climate | 4 | 55 | 88 | 23 | 12 | 3.09 | |
| | Employee satisfaction | 1 | 31 | 116 | 31 | 5 | 2.96 | |

Fig. 2   Satisfaction Degree for the Effect of Process Reform.

Satisfaction degree = 5: Very satisfied, 4: Somewhat satisfied, 3: Fair, 2: Somewhat not satisfied, 1: Not satisfied at all.

| Korean Enterprise | Item | Satisfaction Degree | | | | | Average | Average of Each Group |
|---|---|---|---|---|---|---|---|---|
| | | 5 | 4 | 3 | 2 | 1 | | |
| Financial | Sales | 15 | 40 | 35 | 6 | 1 | 3.64 | 3.55 |
| | Cost effectiveness | 9 | 39 | 41 | 9 | 0 | 3.49 | |
| | Selling cost | 5 | 36 | 44 | 13 | 0 | 3.34 | |
| | General and administrative expenses | 9 | 46 | 37 | 4 | 2 | 3.57 | |
| | Production cost | 12 | 52 | 26 | 6 | 1 | 3.70 | |
| Customer | Customer satisfaction | 15 | 52 | 23 | 7 | 0 | 3.77 | 3.53 |
| | Market share | 8 | 34 | 48 | 6 | 2 | 3.41 | |
| | Customer fixing rate | 10 | 30 | 49 | 7 | 2 | 3.40 | |
| Internal process | Cycle time | 14 | 41 | 36 | 5 | 1 | 3.64 | 3.66 |
| | Return rate and claim | 11 | 39 | 38 | 7 | 2 | 3.52 | |
| | Ratio to keep appointed date of delivery | 15 | 48 | 30 | 3 | 0 | 3.78 | |
| | Quantity of inventory | 16 | 49 | 24 | 6 | 2 | 3.73 | |
| | Productivity of indirect section | 8 | 53 | 30 | 6 | 0 | 3.65 | |
| Learning and growth | Awareness of employees for changes | 12 | 57 | 20 | 9 | 0 | 3.73 | 3.39 |
| | Paradigm and climate | 9 | 54 | 27 | 7 | 1 | 3.64 | |
| | Employee satisfaction | 3 | 44 | 40 | 10 | 1 | 3.39 | |

Fig. 2   (*Continued*).

The total averages of satisfaction degree of Japanese and Korean enterprises are 3.04 and 3.59 respectively. This means that the Korean satisfaction degree is higher than the Japanese one. This variance must be investigated very carefully considering the difference in styles in replying to such a questionnaire in the two countries. Namely, we should not simply assume that the Korean satisfaction degree is higher than the Japanese one. However, the columns in which the sub-total of "5: Very satisfied" and "4: Somewhat satisfied" is bigger than the sub-total of "3: Fair", "2: Somewhat not satisfied" and "1: Not satisfied at all" are displayed with gray color. Although the number of gray colored columns is only one in Japanese enterprises, the number is eleven in Korean enterprises.

The entries with the highest satisfaction degree in Japanese enterprises were "reduction of production cost" (3.35), "enhancement of appointed date of delivery" (3.29), and "enhancement of customer satisfaction" (3.25). In Korean enterprises, it was the "enhancement of appointed date of delivery" (3.78), "enhancement of customer satisfaction" (3.77), "reduction of inventory" (3.73), "consciousness enhancement of an employee for a change" (3.73). Business process reform does not generate much effect from the viewpoint of the customer such as increasing the ratio of fixed customers and market share totally.

In addition, as for the Japanese enterprise, the satisfaction degree of process reform is high for production cost reduction, but for other finance categories is not high. The satisfaction degree of Korean enterprises regarding the increase of sales besides production cost reduction are quite high, however the process reform does not contribute to the whole financial indexes. On the other hand, 1.1–6.0% of Japanese enterprises and 5.1–15.5% of Korean enterprises are satisfied with the finance result and/or customer viewpoint.

## 4.3   *Relationship between process reform and the effect*

Figure 3 shows the result of a chi-square test based on the cross tabulation for the relationship between the degree of process reform and the satisfaction degree. The numerical value in the cell represents meaningful probability (Monte Carlo both sides significant probability), and the plaited cell with gray color shows intentionality by 5% level of significance. From this result, the satisfaction degree is high if the enterprise progress provides sufficient reform of business processes.

In Japanese enterprises, sales increase if there is a satisfaction degree of reform for "production process", "physical distribution process", "after-sales service" and "alliance process". On the other hand, selling costs decrease if there is a satisfaction degree for the reform of the "warehouse

| Japanese Enterprises | | Procurement | R&D | Manufacturing | Warehouse Management | Physical Distribution | Sale and After Service | Administration | Alliance | Recycle |
|---|---|---|---|---|---|---|---|---|---|---|
| Financial | Sales | 0.052 | 0.664 | 0.000 | 0.236 | 0.035 | 0.049 | 0.244 | 0.017 | 0.766 |
| | Cost effectiveness | 0.166 | 0.053 | 0.053 | 0.442 | 0.122 | 0.110 | 0.336 | 0.239 | 0.233 |
| | Selling cost | 0.123 | 0.379 | 0.231 | 0.032 | 0.352 | 0.774 | 0.048 | 0.309 | 0.559 |
| | General and administrative expenses | 0.033 | 0.617 | 0.029 | 0.082 | 0.248 | 0.680 | 0.005 | 0.320 | 0.862 |
| | Production cost | 0.045 | 0.208 | 0.001 | 0.022 | 0.117 | 0.121 | 0.113 | 0.228 | 0.272 |
| Customer | Customer satisfaction | 0.004 | 0.698 | 0.352 | 0.117 | 0.145 | 0.147 | 0.065 | 0.239 | 0.469 |
| | Market share | 0.017 | 0.279 | 0.309 | 0.482 | 0.455 | 0.034 | 0.116 | 0.108 | 0.288 |
| | Customer fixing rate | 0.221 | 0.531 | 0.043 | 0.772 | 0.393 | 0.125 | 0.453 | 0.611 | 0.801 |
| Internal process | Cycle time | 0.030 | 0.009 | 0.003 | 0.118 | 0.379 | 0.004 | 0.241 | 0.355 | 0.024 |
| | Return rate and claim | 0.133 | 0.142 | 0.777 | 0.002 | 0.093 | 0.322 | 0.422 | 0.369 | 0.276 |
| | Ratio to keep appointed date of delivery | 0.007 | 0.108 | 0.069 | 0.009 | 0.110 | 0.027 | 0.382 | 0.106 | 0.081 |
| | Quantity of inventory | 0.100 | 0.573 | 0.003 | 0.001 | 0.003 | 0.237 | 0.173 | 0.694 | 0.430 |
| | Productivity of indirect section | 0.378 | 0.059 | 0.017 | 0.311 | 0.060 | 0.192 | 0.000 | 0.147 | 0.494 |
| Learning and growth | Awareness of employees for changes | 0.006 | 0.001 | 0.001 | 0.131 | 0.453 | 0.100 | 0.179 | 0.390 | 0.080 |
| | Paradigm and climate | 0.003 | 0.003 | 0.003 | 0.068 | 0.504 | 0.002 | 0.313 | 0.905 | 0.833 |
| | Employee satisfaction | 0.052 | 0.002 | 0.014 | 0.703 | 0.065 | 0.000 | 0.159 | 0.536 | 0.020 |

Fig. 3    Degree of Process Reform and Satisfaction Degree.

| Korean Enterprises | | Procurement | R&D | Manufacturing | Warehouse Management | Physical Distribution | After Service | Sale and Administration | Alliance | Recycle | Sales |
|---|---|---|---|---|---|---|---|---|---|---|---|
| Financial | Sales | 0.003 | 0.125 | 0.149 | 0.322 | 0.174 | 0.198 | 0.467 | 0.090 | 0.015 | 0.400 |
| | Cost effectiveness | 0.640 | 0.151 | 0.070 | 0.152 | 0.268 | 0.062 | 0.004 | 0.008 | 0.022 | 0.175 |
| | Selling cost | 0.002 | 0.134 | 0.029 | 0.021 | 0.092 | 0.478 | 0.049 | 0.097 | 0.001 | 0.068 |
| | General and administrative expenses | 0.028 | 0.913 | 0.135 | 0.226 | 0.119 | 0.403 | 0.024 | 0.035 | 0.584 | 0.635 |
| | Production cost | 0.010 | 0.012 | 0.019 | 0.602 | 0.087 | 0.201 | 0.004 | 0.266 | 0.097 | 0.921 |
| Customer | Customer satisfaction | 0.001 | 0.272 | 0.042 | 0.344 | 0.089 | 0.054 | 0.079 | 0.730 | 0.058 | 0.088 |
| | Market share | 0.013 | 0.047 | 0.535 | 0.229 | 0.631 | 0.140 | 0.420 | 0.016 | 0.024 | 0.289 |
| | Customer fixing rate | 0.006 | 0.018 | 0.296 | 0.186 | 0.127 | 0.018 | 0.099 | 0.045 | 0.189 | 0.145 |
| Internal process | Cycle time | 0.002 | 0.001 | 0.267 | 0.006 | 0.003 | 0.028 | 0.011 | 0.113 | 0.003 | 0.007 |
| | Return rate and claim | 0.165 | 0.857 | 0.732 | 0.488 | 0.335 | 0.401 | 0.979 | 0.457 | 0.089 | 0.104 |
| | Ratio to keep appointed date of delivery | 0.004 | 0.034 | 0.030 | 0.027 | 0.054 | 0.198 | 0.036 | 0.326 | 0.012 | 0.086 |
| | Quantity of inventory | 0.052 | 0.086 | 0.854 | 0.166 | 0.028 | 0.714 | 0.325 | 0.404 | 0.043 | 0.770 |
| | Productivity of indirect section | 0.031 | 0.357 | 0.086 | 0.027 | 0.001 | 0.085 | 0.001 | 0.016 | 0.010 | 0.205 |
| Learning and growth | Awareness of employees for changes | 0.011 | 0.137 | 0.071 | 0.622 | 0.808 | 0.091 | 0.002 | 0.579 | 0.115 | 0.003 |
| | Paradigm and climate | 0.000 | 0.030 | 0.112 | 0.172 | 0.057 | 0.002 | 0.000 | 0.406 | 0.088 | 0.002 |
| | Employee satisfaction | 0.012 | 0.177 | 0.115 | 0.301 | 0.259 | 0.295 | 0.030 | 0.387 | 0.001 | 0.066 |

Fig. 3 (*Continued*)

management process" and "administration process". As a whole, the reform of production process and procurement process are linked to the effect of finance and customer satisfaction.

On the contrary, in Korean enterprises, the effect for the reform of the procurement process is clearly recognized, along with the satisfaction degree for the viewpoints of finance and customer satisfaction. In addition, the reform of "production process", "administration process", and "recycle process" led to the effect of finance and customer satisfaction. It is noted that the contribution of the reform of the "research and development process" becomes high compared with the Japanese enterprises.

## 5 Examination Based on the BSC Framework

The outcomes of business process innovation have been examined based on the BSC framework. Categorical regression analysis was applied to investigate the causal relationship among the satisfactory items of four groups: financial, customer, inner process and learning & growth. We have analyzed which item has the biggest contribution ratio for satisfactory items using the correlation coefficient. The analyzed result is shown in Figures 4 and 5.

Regarding Japanese enterprises, "enhancement of cycle time" of the process viewpoint has a direct correlation with the "awareness of employees for changes", "paradigm and climate" and "employee satisfaction" in the learning and development viewpoints. The multiple correlation coefficient is 0.656. The percentage contribution of "paradigm and climate" is high at 0.617. In other words, the enterprise with good "paradigm and climate" tends to be high "enhancement of cycle time". On the other hand "reduction of inventory" has a weak correlation with these three items of the learning and development viewpoint. In addition, there is a causation between the business process and customer satisfaction, because "enhancement of customer satisfaction" is achieved if "appointed date of delivery" and "productivity of indirect section" are improved. Furthermore, "to keep appointed date of delivery" influences "market share" and "to reduce return rate and claim" contributes to "customer fixing rate". Strong causation between viewpoints of customer and finance is recognized. Namely, market share influences sales amount, cost effectiveness, selling cost and general and administrative expenses just as customer fixing rate influences customer fixing rate. However, "reduction of production cost" is weak in causation for each item in the viewpoint of the customer and strong for

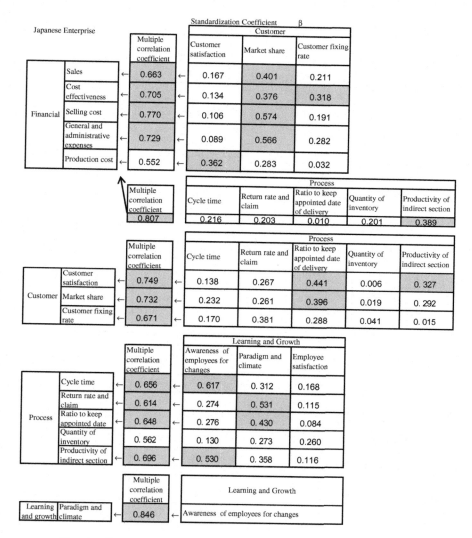

Fig. 4   Categorical Regression Analysis for Japanese Enterprises.

each item in the viewpoint of business process (especially "productivity of indirect section"). Process reform is performed especially for reduction of production cost in Japanese enterprises.

In Korean enterprises, "paradigm and climate" influences "enhancement of cycle time" and the "ratio to keep appointed date of delivery".

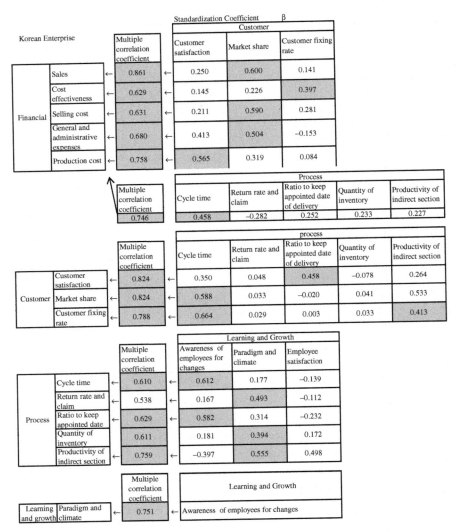

Fig. 5    Categorical Regression Analysis for Korean Enterprises.

In addition, "enhancement of employee satisfaction degree" has high correlation with "reduction of inventory" and "productivity improvement of indirect section". On the other hand, three items of viewpoint of learning and development have week correlation with "deterioration of return rate/claim" of viewpoint of process. There is a causal sequence between the viewpoints of process and customer, and "to keep appointed date of delivery" greatly influences the "customer satisfaction". Furthermore, "enhancement of cycle time" influences the "enhancement of market share" and "enhancement of customer fixing rate". In addition, there is strong correlation between viewpoints of customer and finance, and it is found that "enhancement of market share" influences "increase of sales", "enhancement of cost-effectiveness", and "deterioration of general and administrative expenses". The enhancement of "customer fixing rate" contributes to the "deterioration of selling cost", and "enhancement of customer satisfaction" contributes to "reduction of production cost".

On the basis of the above analysis, the causation of each item is illustrated in Figures 6 and 7. Results of business process management have effects on the financial results in the end. Correlation to customer viewpoint was high for "increase of sales" and "reduction of production cost" in Korean enterprises, and low for "deterioration of selling cost", "deterioration of general and administrative expenses", and "enhancement of cost-effectiveness" in Japanese enterprise. In addition, in Korean enterprises, the correlation of viewpoints of the process and the customer's, is quite high. Furthermore, there is a difference in that "enhancement of cycle time" is very effective in Korean enterprises, but the "enhancement of appointed date of delivery" and "decrease of return rate and claim" are effective in Japanese enterprises. Each item in the viewpoints of process and learning and growth has the same correlation in Japanese and Korean enterprises. In addition, items in the viewpoint of learning and growth have weak correlation with "return rate and claim" in Korean enterprises, but with "inventory cost" in Japanese enterprises.

## 6    Important Processes in Near Future

"Procurement process", "research and development process", and "production process" are important for Japanese enterprises as shown in Figure 8. Japanese enterprises consider that process reform has a significant effect in the reduction of production cost and enhancement of efficiency of enterprise inside processes.

On the other hand, "research and development process", "production process" and "physical distribution process" are important for Korean enterprises. Korean enterprises consider that process reform has much effect in enhancement of customer satisfaction and increase of sales in

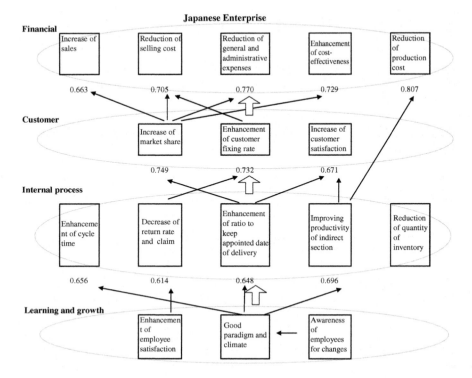

Fig. 6   Map of Causal Relationship between Satisfactory Items for Japanese Enterprises.

addition to reduction of production cost. To achieve these process reforms, creative paradigm changes are necessary. This greatly affects employee satisfaction.

## Summary

The degree of process reform and its outcomes has been analyzed based on the survey results of Japanese and Korean companies. Furthermore, the relationship between BPM and BSC (the Balanced Scorecard) has been discussed here.

In Japanese enterprises, sales increase if there is a satisfactory degree of reform of "production process", "physical distribution process", "after-sales service" and "alliance process". On the other hand, sales costs decrease if there is a satisfactory degree of reform of "warehouse management

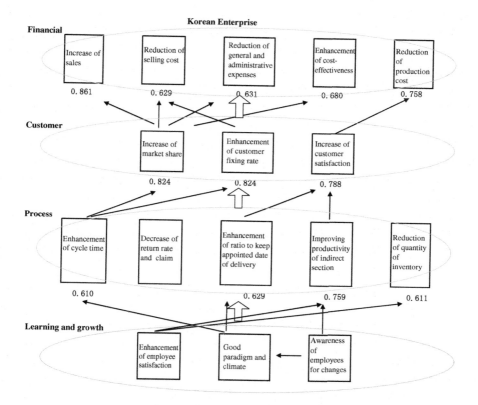

Fig. 7   Map of Causal Relationship between Satisfactory Items for Korean Enterprises.

process" and "administration process". On the contrary, in Korean enterprises, the effects of reform of the procurement process are clearly recognized, and almost all of the indexes in the viewpoints of finance and customer are satisfactory.

The customer viewpoint has a high correlation with the "increase of sales" and "reduction of production cost" in Korean enterprises, with a low correlation for "deterioration of selling cost", "deterioration of general and administrative expenses" and "enhancement of cost-effectiveness" in Japanese enterprise. In addition, the correlation of the viewpoints of process and customer is quite high in Korean enterprise.

We can clearly see how the BPM affects financial results by the categorical regression analysis with the framework of BSC. Management

| Process | Japanese Enterprises | | Korean Enterprises | |
|---|---|---|---|---|
| Procurement | 87 | 15.70% | 27 | 9.10% |
| R&D | 157 | 28.40% | 64 | 21.60% |
| Manufacturing | 129 | 23.30% | 60 | 20.30% |
| Warehouse management | 9 | 1.60% | 2 | 0.70% |
| Physical distribution | 47 | 8.50% | 36 | 12.20% |
| After service | 36 | 6.50% | 26 | 8.80% |
| Administration | 40 | 7.20% | 22 | 7.40% |
| Alliance | 40 | 7.20% | 16 | 5.40% |
| Recycle | 8 | 1.40% | 5 | 1.70% |
| Sale | — | — | 38 | 12.80% |
| Total | 553 | | 296 | |

Fig. 8    Important Processes for Dominant Competition.

strategy is important. However, we can know which process should be better improved by this categorical regression analysis based on current findings. This is a very powerful tool to support decision-making.

## References

Kaplan, R.S. and D.P. Norton. (1992). The Balanced Scorecard: Measures that Drive Performance, *Harvard Business Review*, 70(1).

Kaplan, R.S. and D.P. Norton. (1996). *The Balanced Scorecard: Translating Strategy into Action*, Harvard Business School Press.

Lee, G.Y., M. Kosuga and Y. Nagasaka. (2006). *Strategic Process Management — Theory and Practice*, Zeimukeirikyokai. (In Japanese)

Mintzberg, H. (1978). Patterns in Strategy Formulation, *Management Science*, 24(9), pp. 934–948.

Monden Y. (2002). *The Introduction to Empirical Research of Accounting and Management: Analysis of Corporate Model by SPSS*, ChuoKeizai Co. (In Japanese)

Monden Y. and G.Y. Lee. (2005). Conceptual Framework and Management Accounting of Process Management, *Accounting*, Chuokeizai Co., 57(5), pp. 18–25. (In Japanese)

Nagasaka Y. and K. Sakate. (2005). Investigation of Process Management in Japanese Companies, *Accounting*, Chuokeizai Co., 57(5), pp. 33–41. (In Japanese)

# About the Volume Editors

## Gunyung Lee

Professor, Faculty of Economics, Niigata University, Japan

Majoring in Cost and Management Accounting

BA from Sogang University, Korea, MBA and Ph.D. from Tsukuba University, Japan

### Main Publications

Japanese Management Style in Achieving the Cost Reduction Targets. In *Japanese Cost Management*, Y. Monden, ed. London: Imperial College Press, 2000, Chapter 18.

*Strategic Process Management* (Research Project Series No.4). Lee, G.Y., M. Kosuga and Y. Nagasaka, eds., 2006. Japanese Association of Management Accounting. (In Japanese).

*Value-Based Management of the Rising Sun.* Monden, Y., K. Miyamoto, K. Hamada, G. Y. Lee and T. Asada, eds. Singapore: World Scientific Co., 2006.

The Framework of Business Process Management and Dell Computers (co-author). In *Japanese Management Accounting Today*, Monden, Y., M. Kosuga, Y. Nagasaka, S. Hiraoka and N. Hoshi, eds., pp. 235–248. Singapore: World Scientific Co. 2007.

The Usefulness of Business Process Management in Cost Management (co-author). *The Journal of Cost Accounting Research* (Japan Cost Accounting Association), 33(1), 2009, pp. 18–27. (In Japanese).

## Masanobu Kosuga

Professor, School of Business Administration, Kwansei Gakuin University, Japan

Majoring in Cost and Management Accounting

BA, MBA, and Ph.D. from Kwansei Gakuin University

## Main Publications

*Behavioral Theory of Budgeting* (2nd Ed.). Tokyo: Chuou-Keizai-Sha, Inc. 1997. (In Japanese).

*Fundamental of Cost Accounting.* Tokyo: Chuou-Keizai-Sha, Inc. 1999. (In Japanese).

*An Introduction to Management Accounting.* Miyamoto, K. and M. Kosuga, eds. Tokyo: Chuou-Keizai-Sha, Inc. 2006. (In Japanese).

*Strategic Process Management* (Research Project Series No. 4). Lee, G.Y., M. Kosuga and Y. Nagasaka, eds. Japanese Association of Management Accounting 2006. (In Japanese).

*An Introduction to Cost Accounting.* Tokyo: Chuou-Keizai-Sha, Inc. 2007. (In Japanese).

*Japanese Management Accounting Today.* Monden, Y., M. Kosuga, Y. Nagasaka, S. Hiraoka and N. Hoshi, eds. Singapore: World Scientific Pub. Co. 2007.

*Management Accounting: Standard Text.* Tokyo: Chuou-Keizai-Sha, Inc. 2008. (In Japanese) (co-editor).

## Yoshiyuki Nagasaka

Professor, Faculty of Business Administration, Konan University, Japan

Majoring in Management Accounting and Management Information

Bachelor of Engineering, Master of Engineering and Doctor of Engineering from Osaka University

## Main Publications

Cost Reduction Approach to Manufacturing Administrative Departments in a Japanese industry machinery manufacturer. In *Japanese Cost Management*, Monden, Y., ed. London: Imperial College Press 2000, Chapter 15.

IT and Process Innovation in Japanese Enterprise (co-author). In *Value-Based Management of the Rising Sun*, Monden, Y., K. Miyamoto, K. Hamada, G.Y. Lee and T. Asada, eds. Singapore: World Scientific Pub. Co. 2006, Chapter 30.

*Japanese Management Accounting Today.* Monden, Y., M. Kosuga, Y. Nagasaka, S. Hiraoka, and N. Hoshi. Singapore: World Scientific Co. 2007.

Automation and Process Management in Foundry. *International Journal of Automation Technology*, 2(4), 2008, pp. 266–275.

# Byungkyu Sohn

Professor, College of Business Administration, Sookmyung Women's University

Majoring in Supply Chain Management

BA from Seoul National University, Korea, MBA from KAIST (Korea Advanced Institute of Science and Technology), Korea, and from Bowling Green State University, USA, Ph.D. from Michigan State University, USA.

## Main Publications

*A Study on Applying MSA of U. S. to Korean Procurement Bureau (co-author).* The Korean Bureau of Procurement 2003. (In Korean).

*Foundation of Operations Management.* Sohn, B.K., J.Y. Kang, D.K. Min, J.H. Park and Y.D. Won, eds. Seoul: Sigma Press 2004. (In Korean).

Information Sharing between Buying Firms and Suppliers and the Efficiency of Production Planning. *Journal of Economics and Management,* 33(2), 2003, pp. 87–110. (In Korean).

A Study on SCM Strategy of Korean Discount Retailers: Comparison between E-Mart and Homeplus (co-author). *Journal of Economics and Management,* 34(2), 2005, pp. 145–164. (In Korean).

Purchasing Function as a New Competitive Weapon. *Journal of Economics and Management,* 36, 2006, pp. 181–196. (In Korean).

A Study on Customer-Centered Business Process Strategy of Korean Firms (co-author). In *Strategic Process Management* (Research Project Series No. 4), Lee, G.Y., M. Kosuga and Y. Nagasaka, eds. Japanese Association of Management Accounting 2006, Chapter 10. (In Japanese).

# Index